"Seven women friends meet fo  They encourage each other to i up for each other's readings, and buy each other's books. *Rethinking the Ground Rules* is the second book they wrote together, coming after *An Apple in Her Hand*. Raucous and mesmerizing, the texts included in this collection are spellbinding, electrifying, honest, uplifting, life-affirming, and pure delight."

— *Lucia Cherciu, Author of Train Ride to Bucharest,*
Poet Laureate of Dutchess County

"The Hudson Valley Women's Writing Group exposes their truths, no holding back! They masterfully meld honesty and heart. Memories are rediscovered inhabiting places where the potent smells of coal, cow dung, oil, grass rise. Now my heart too wishes to design a museum to enshrine not what was but what was wished for. As I am transported alongside a grandfather gleefully kissing the earth while resurrecting bud and bloom with his grit-filled arthritic hands, I feel his joy. You will be absorbed into the stories in these varied works. I know an uplifting transformation of Spirit will occur for you as it has for me."

— *Jerrice J. Baptiste, Poetry Facilitator,*
WKZE Radio Host, Author of Wintry Mix

"7 writers/9 chapters/1 book. *Rethinking the Ground Rules* does more than make us rethink. This volume with its journey through poems, both formal and free form; prose memoir, essay and hybrid writing gives us a chance to reorder our priorities. And to meditate on those things important to us which we have for the moment (or the past months) misplaced or felt that we have lost. It may bear witness to a darkened world, but then opens doors through which the light of our lives shines through. As readers, we should think beyond the idea of anthology and experience a cohesive, interconnected work from the ideas, the hearts and the free rein creativity of these gifted writers. The reader will be rewarded by revisiting often."

Laurence Carr, Author of Paradise Loft
and Lightwoodpress.com

RETHINKING
THE GROUND *Rules*

Works by the Hudson Valley Women's Writing Group
Kappa Waugh, Jan Zlotnik Schmidt, Mary K O'Melveny,
Tana Miller, Eileen Howard, Kit Goldpaugh, Colleen Geraghty

MediacsBooks

36 Henry W. Dubois Dr., #8
New Paltz, New York 12561
mediacsbooks.com

Cover Design by Elaine Norman
Interior Design by Abby Carola

Rethinking The Ground Rules
ISBN 978-1-7358460-6-4

Table of Contents

**Chapter 3: Honoring Craft: From Villanelles
    to Golden Shovels**

**Chapter 4: Mythology and Spirituality:
    Known and Unknown Gods**

Chapter 5: Tales of the Natural World

Chapter 6: Pandemic Reflections and Reactions

CHAPTER 1

Breaking the Rules

What Does This Old Woman Want Now?

Tana Miller

she waltzes naked past her next-door neighbor's house
he throws down his hedge-clippers   cheers *hurrah hurrah*
she blows him kisses   ample hips sway   bosoms jiggle
a smile flickers on her lips as she passes the next house
pretends not to see the busy-body gawking behind her lace curtains
turns left   meanders along the road leading to the village   no rush
bends to examine this season's gift: a clump of lavender dame's rocket
she marks her life by wildflowers: daisies orange ditch lilies
chicory Queen Anne's lace goldenrod   a holy book of her days
her ample flesh quivers with joy   bounces   bings   she swings
her arms   scratches a zoftig buttock   does not rein
in her round belly ball   lets her bare feet flap flap
a red pickup truck with a baseball-cap-wearing driver approaches
veers onto the shoulder   swerves back   brakes
shouts   *you go girl*   lays on his horn as he guns his engine
she throws her head back   laughing   waves
a squirrel   winter-thin   darts in front of her
dives into the bushes   the squirrel passes no judgement
on her unclothed flesh   nor do the brambles along the road
nor the stones nor the green-smelling trees   they don't seem to notice
at the village's edge she rests on a bench   an older man
walking a pug dog past the bench pauses abruptly   staring
the dog wags his stubby tail   the man coughs   stumbles on
her plump thighs nestle together   she tips her head back
closes her eyes   lets the sun warm her face
red spangly lines dance behind her eyelids
as she dozes deep within the world's embrace

The Visit
Kappa Waugh

My mother's college roommate phoned her and suggested a visit. Should she come alone or bring the five children and the nanny? "Oh, come alone!" my mother replied. "Such fun; we'll be able to talk over Mt. Holyoke days and all the gossip since!"

We had heard stories about Nora Coulter. Smart, funny, she had come back to the dorm after dates, always pushing the curfew, grass all over her clothes. We were too young to interpret this as sex in the bushes, but thought of Nora as someone who romped. Her husband, referred to by my mother as 'Geoffrey the Nazi,' would not be coming, nor her lecherous father-in-law, who, according to my mother, pinched her bottom and chased her around the dining room table. We thought Nora sounded swell and looked forward to the visit.

She arrived on a hot Virginia day with no nanny and the five children. Geoff Jr. was dark and brooding, eight years old, just a bit older than my brother Douglass. Next came Jessica, a beautiful girl with blond pigtails, seven like me. Twin boys, let's call them Smith and Wesson since I have forgotten their names, and they were a pair of trained killers at four. Bringing up the rear was Baby Betsy, an infant girl with a stye. Housing six additional people was a challenge; Nora and the baby went in the guest room. My oldest brother, Robin, was away for the weekend, due to return near the end of the visit, so his bedroom went to Geoffrey Jr. Jessica was billeted with me, and my mother's sense of Southern hospitality meant Jessica got my bed while I slept on the floor. The twins shared the day bed in my father's study. This last amazed me, since we children were only allowed in there for short periods, as my father kept a messy office with precarious piles of paper and books, in a system known only to him.

All went well the first evening. Everyone was on best behavior, and we children were still sizing each other up. The first sign of horrors to come was my mother telling me to fetch my pillow for Betsy. As the youngest child I was always last in line for new things; the hand-me-down policy was strictly followed in my family. By some fluke I had received a pillow from my grandmother. Not exactly a new pillow, but it did not have the dark brown drool marks, the pricking pinfeathers, the smell of generations of sleepers. I was immensely possessive of it. It was way too fine for a baby with a stye. Furthermore, Betsy seemed to subsist on candy corn.

I could hardly tell where the seeping from the stye ended, and the candy corn dribble began. Despite my fierce protests, my mother put the shoulder vise on me, and I had to give in. The vise was a move she had perfected to save everyone the shame of a mother publicly coercing her child. Her fingers would meet, pinching under my collarbone, as she asked sweetly, "You'd be happy to share your pillow with Betsy, wouldn't you Katharine?" Listing slightly toward the pinch, I succumbed and answered yes.

The next day, Saturday, we set out, as with all our visitors, to take them around Colonial Williamsburg. The mothers walked ahead, chattering away. So far we had seen none of Nora's sporting qualities. She seemed vague, preoccupied, as if she were watching a movie we couldn't see. Geoff was sulky, kicking at flowers and pulling off their heads. Jessica walked beside me confiding in me how sad it was that my parents had adopted me and had received such an ugly child in the bargain. It had never really occurred to me that I was adopted, but then I remembered my mother's tales of childbirth. "Oh, they gave me a shot of something, then I woke up and there you were. Honestly, they could have foisted anybody's baby on me!" Jessica seemed at first sympathetic. "Don't worry; lots of kids are adopted, and they almost always get along ok. Of course, it's not like having your real parents. And it usually means something was wrong with your actual mother that she had to give you away. But maybe it was just because you were such an ugly baby. You're lucky the Adairs took you in."

I had seen baby pictures of myself, but sure enough, it was always my grandmother holding me, not my mother. The one picture of her with me as a solemn baby did not look happy. I ran ahead to ask my mother if I had been adopted. "Don't be ridiculous!" It was her standard reply to many of our questions, and, in my experience, had mostly to do with not wanting to deal with it, and little to do with the true answer.

I went back to Jessica and told her my mother had said it was ridiculous. "Oh they always wait to tell you at some special time." Jessica dropped behind and stepped on the heels of my sandals, making them

4

come off. This involved stopping, removing them altogether, unbuckling them, putting them on, and rebuckling them. The first time I thought it was an accident, and hurried to catch up. But she did it a number of times, so we got quite far behind. When my mother noticed, she told me to stop dawdling. Jessica put her arm around my shoulders, saying sweetly to my mother, "I know she's younger; I'll keep her from getting lost."

This kind of psychological warfare went on all day. My mother liked us to shine before visitors and was irritated with my dragging and whining. The injustice of it soon had me as sullen as Geoff Jr. The twins were quickly bored by the historical sights. Once the cannon was set off and the muskets fired, they began complaining. "We hate the buildings." "The costumes are stupid." "Why can't we have guns?" "We want to shoot the cannon." Nora tried to appease them with spears from a souvenir stand. For the rest of the walk they goosed and poked Douglass and me, which brought a rare smile to Geoff's face.

In the evening during cocktail hour, the four oldest Hill kids ganged up on Douglass and me upstairs and started physically attacking us. We didn't know what to do. All the house rules of hospitality, of silence during cocktails, of not bothering our parents, of not tattling, left us defenseless. Later my mother told us she heard the crashing, but when she suggested they check on us, Nora said it was surely just the children horsing around. At dinnertime Geoff was quiet and Jessica sparkled. What a nice visit they were having, what lovely children Douglass and I were. What an interesting town was Williamsburg.

At church the next morning, my mother, by habit, tried to separate the children as much as possible. Douglass and I could set each other off, snorting and giggling. But Jessica asked if she couldn't please sit next to her new best friend. When I whispered no to my mother, she hissed back, "Don't be disagreeable." Jessica pinched me throughout the service, while managing to look angelic. My jumps and starts earned a, "Stop fidgeting!" from my mother.

While my mother tried to get Sunday dinner on the table, the twins kept running through the kitchen, goosing her with their spears. On the third circuit, my mother tripped them both and told them she'd hate to have an accident with boiling water. By lunch time the marks from Saturday night's fight and Jessica's Sunday pinches matured into purple bruises up and down my arms. "What happened to your arms, Katharine?" my mother asked. "Oh, I got bumped at church," I replied, as true as I could be to the unspoken rule to protect the grownups from the uglier aspects of childhood.

But when my brother Robin, a big boy of eleven, came home that afternoon, Douglass and I filled his ears with tales of the Hill children's attacks. That afternoon, before they left, we trapped our little visitors in Robin's bedroom, where we beat them up as thoroughly as we could. Geoffrey turned out to be claustrophobic, so Robin barricaded him in the closet, leaving him banging and pleading for release. He then balanced the twins' spears out of reach on the curtain rod and told them in inventive detail how many ways he would use the spears "under their clothes, where it wouldn't show." Douglass and I threw Jessica back and forth, slamming her into furniture, slapping her each time. My mother told us later she had eventually figured out what was happening, so when Nora finally decided to go up and investigate the sounds of mayhem, my mother stopped her with, "Oh, it's just the children roughhousing."

When I retrieved my pillow, it was stiff with Betsy's exudings, even under a clean pillowcase, and it smelled utterly alien.

Fisher Queen
Colleen Geraghty

Stunned silent by the maiden's light. Crimson crown,
sunlit beauty. Radiant hands swooping, soaring
bridging earth and heaven.
Peace doves fly from her sun-kissed lips–a benediction.
Her heartbeats winnow through
a rutting sea of lies. She unwinds the clock
and winds it again. Amazing the grace
the maiden bestows. She shapeshifts to cormorant
plunging deep into dark waters – never unclean
as the old gods declared,
bold as an overripe plum, ancient as a sturdy oak,
flexible as a feather–all at once
and everything.
Blessed be the Fisher Queen,
the storytellers' goddess inhaling mysteries of the dark moon.
Winged maiden diving deep, spinning new light.
She shapeshifts insufferable divides!
Her salt glands run deep. She exhales
possibilities, sets the inaugural dawn aflame.

*This poem was written as a tribute to Amanda Gorman

Naked Faculty Action Figures
Kit Goldpaugh

Everybody is talking at once, who traveled where, who got married, divorced, gave birth, had cosmetic surgery, who lost weight. It's the first day of school, the first Tuesday in September, the day before the students arrive, technically, a superintendent's training day. The faculty is filing into the middle school library. We've been going all morning.

At 7:45, every teacher in the district assembled in the high school auditorium to pledge the flag, sing "The Star Spangled Banner," meet the new faculty and knock off two mandatory topics: sexual harassment in the work place and protocols for handling blood borne pathogens. Both sessions are as awful as anticipated, the same role playing and the same circa 1980 latex gloves and bleach movie. When the sex and blood part of the day ended, teachers had forty-five minutes to enjoy lunch before returning to individual schools. That's where we are now.

"Welcome back. I hope everyone had a good summer. I know that you're all eager to get to your classrooms, so let's get to business and we'll have you out of here by two. I think I've met most of you but if not, I am Todd Davidson, and I'm looking forward to getting to know all of you over the upcoming year."

Principal Todd looks about fifteen in his bar-mitzvah suit and tie. I feel one hundred. "We'll start this afternoon with a little warm up activity. When I click the lights, I want you to line up alphabetically by your favorite author's last name."

Who wrote *Fifty Shades of Grey?* Who wrote *Mr. Popper's Penguins?* Did Betty Crocker write her own book?

Lie, I think. Nobody cares. John Grisham. Steven King. We're in a library. Jesus on a pogo stick! Look at a book jacket and claim its author. Stand anywhere so we can get back to our classrooms! What I say is, "I like Margaret Atwood, and I like Emily Bronte and I like Zora Neale Hurston, and I like Betty Smith. I still love Tolkien." I point. We scurry around. Principal Davidson seems pleased with our cooperation.

I turn to my teammate and say, "Twenty dollars says he offers us this warm-up for our own classes." But Mike doesn't take the bet because he hates to lose. Principal Davidson clicks the lights, and we freeze like Pavlovian poodles. "Please take a seat." Sit. Stay. "Feel free to use this warm-up in your own classes." I kick Mike. "I see that you've noticed index cards on the table. I want each of you to take a card." He clasps his hands, "We all start the year with hopes and goals and wishes." He draws a deep breath, "I want each of you to take a minute and write down a wish or hope you have for the year ahead. Or more than one."

Immediately I write: "I wish this goddamn meeting would end, so I could finish setting up my classroom. I hope that all my students are mute and sedated. I kind of wish someone would kill me. I wish for a snow day tomorrow." I'm writing furiously now. The lights blink. We freeze.

"Now pass your card to the person on your right."

Years later at our union retirement party, I was introduced as the teacher that nobody wanted to sit next to at a faculty meeting. I stood my full five feet, and nodded slightly, as Kate Middleton Cambridge or Jane Goodall might and mouthed thank you.

Usually during faculty meetings in the library, I'd seek a seat hidden in the stacks where I could quietly grade quizzes or get a little reading in. How I loathed arriving late and having to sit up front where I couldn't even pass notes or play hangman. The year that the state of New York decided to introduce and implement The Core Curriculum, the faculty was taught the curriculum and instructed to follow it with fealty. I remember thinking, what an odd and ominous use of the word. After that, virtually every meeting, whether a superintendent's training day or a ten-person departmental meeting, included an onslaught of vocabulary: standard, tiers, paradigm shift, scaffolded instruction, essential idea, evidence, cogent reasoning, differentiated instruction, anchor papers, rubrics. The obvious choice of entertainment during these hours of professional development was bullshit bingo.

I did not invent bullshit bingo. Bullshit bingo is like regular bingo except the board is filled with all the vocabulary you can predict for an upcoming meeting. During faculty training sessions, the bank contained words and phrases such as challenge, confidence, expectations, available resources in addition to the words provided. Bingo had its drawbacks, of course. On bingo days, my team and I arrived early and claimed the table behind the shelf of short stories. The bingo sheets had to be filled before the meeting started. We had to whisper BINGO and hand out prizes quietly. Soon, lots of people wanted to play, and Principal Davidson didn't believe that we were really reviewing the essential vocabulary and listening carefully to the presentations.

Naked Faculty Action Figures is pretty much what it sounds like. Look at the person to your right. Look at the person to your left. Aside from a purse or riding crop, for example, imagine these folks in the buff. You're playing already! A formal version of the game has rules and calls for eight to ten players. Prior to the faculty meeting, each player selects one playing card numbered ace through ten. On an index card, players write down their number and one prop for the game. For example, Mr. Phillip's card might be seven of hearts, and his prop might be Dorothy's red shoes from *The Wizard of Oz*. His card would say SEVEN, Dorothy's shoes. When the seventh person at the meeting speaks, all players imagine the speaker nude in red shoes.
Mr. Rossini, three of spades, might choose Sally Field's cap from *The Flying Nun* or Russell Crowe's leather jock strap from *Gladiator*. Once everyone at the table has selected a number and a prop, we write both on an index card, the principal clicks the lights, and the game begins.

Nobody has number one because the principal always speaks first, and we've already pictured him naked. The second person to speak today is a diminutive bald headed social studies instructor. At our table, the science teacher has number two, and the prop is Celine Dion's wedding hat. All players at the table then imagine the little social studies teacher naked except for Celine's hat. The third person to speak is the principal's seventy-seven year old secretary. On my card is number three and my prop is a long tail. At this juncture in he game, players are imagining the naked teacher in the hat as well as naked and wrinkled Mrs. Lyons with a tail hanging from her crepe ass. The game continues until all ten cards are played. After that, players are encouraged to trade cards for NFAF play dates or NFAF dominos or NFAF dream dates. The game has infinite possibilities and plausible deniability. The most damning evidence might be an index card with the number nine and "latex hooves" or number four and "Princess Diana's sapphire and pearl choker."

Eventually teachers, custodians, and secretaries in the know would greet one another in the halls and say, "Room 104 in bumblebee fur boots." And the response might be, "...and Room 216 in Winnie the Pooh's little red shirt," like a secret code. Obviously, the rules of the game could be modified for almost any professional gathering.

Not everybody found these games helpful or funny. Some people thought that I was disrespectful and very immature. This is nothing I haven't heard my entire life. One permanently disgruntled teacher suggested that I should put as much time and energy into my teaching as I did these games! (Clearly this woman hadn't seen my class in the middle of kung fu punctuation.) I felt a little defensive. She had a point, of course, but it was hard to take her seriously while she stood there naked except for the ferret scurrying up her legs.

Sounding My Childhood

Eileen Howard

Clickety clack, clickety clack,
a locomotive rolls by.
I lie on my back and listen.
It's rhythmic and soothing,
a comforting sound.

As a teen I ride the rails.
The sound so different up close
inside a box car.
Clackety shrackety. Clackety shrackety.
It is louder more insistent,
the smells are all different.
Coal, cow dung, oil, grass.
You can see through the cracks.
The rails whiz by and the
draft brings more aromas.

Camp Colorado mountains.
The river can rampage
in white water rage:
a never cresting ocean wave
that shows its dominion:
navigate with care.
Wake up to another sound.
Burble gurgle, burble gurgle,
the river ripples serenely,
shimmers and shines.

Go to sleep to the sound
of soughing pines in the wind:
hrushhh hrushhh.
Every campsite a different mix of trees,
a different symphony of wind.
Wind gusts sound like
asthmatic freight trains,
a wild thundering swordsman,

a soft lullaby. They can smell of
pine tar pitch, rain, wind loving pollens,
all mixed in with campfire smoke.

Back home the wind runs wild.
Oklahoma flat lands let it rip.
We sail sheets in the wind. They snap:
whap rap, slap whap rap:
then, whomp! The wind fills our sails.
Feet skim the ground,
nose full of dust and dry grass.
The sun blinds my eyes.
We coast in the wind.

Villanelle for Eve Adams
Mary K O'Melveny

> *Eve Adams (b 1891 [Poland] - d 1943 [Auschwitz]) authored the ground-breaking work, "Lesbian Love," and other books championing women's lives without men. In June 1912, at age 20, she traveled to America on the S.S. Vaderland. At Ellis Island, she changed her name from Chawa Zloczower. In Greenwich Village, she founded a lesbian-friendly tearoom and salon known as "Eve's Hangout," visited by many notable writers and activists, including Emma Goldman and Henry Miller. Her work was branded "indecent." Many of her writings were burned. By 1919, she was surveilled and harassed by the FBI, and J. Edgar Hoover played a key role in her 1927 deportation to Poland. She lived in France for sixteen years, including ten with her lover, German-born cabaret singer Hella Olsein Soldner. Both were arrested in December 1943 in Nice and sent by train to Auschwitz where they are presumed to have perished.*

Wanderlust, they called it back then.
I was twenty when I boarded
my ship to Ellis Island. When

I disembarked, nothing had been
saved of my old life. No hoarded
memories of who I had been

or what was expected. Begin
anew, I promised. Recorded
histories always need a pen –

it can be yours, not theirs. So, spin
your own tales of love rewarded:
sisterhoods of flesh, sweaty skin,

free to roam, dress, speak without men
to hold us back or down. *Sordid,*
Shocking some said. The constant din

could consume a room's oxygen
even without burned books. We hid
what we could, laughed at *Mortal Sins.*
We were accosted by G-men

everywhere. Even my *Torrid*
Village hangout could not keep them

out. I was jailed again, again
and eventually deported
back to Poland, my Jewish kin.

I met the woman I had been
searching for in France. I courted
her, our love fated. Now and then

I reach for dreams that could have been –
times before we were transported
to this place where all hope will end –
my Ellis ship, seas uncharted.

Resisting Erasure with Grace*
Jan Zlotnik Schmidt   *(About Bess Houdini)*

At first she only spoke in small words, small letters. Words like puffs of air or flecked stitches on a china doll's bodice. The cloth rumpled by her breath. She only spoke in these words because she was so small, so tiny, so given to erasure.

She took baby steps too, facing the churning world--living with a host of magic men. First she stepped onto a stage in a ruffled tutu and stockings. Pointing her toes in a cake walk dance. Miniature versions of herself she thought. Then into the magic box she went. Cloaked, closed in darkness. She knew what a mummy must have felt wrapped in loose strips of linen, enclosing a body, eyes, nose, mouth--a muffled afterlife. She knew what it meant to jump out of darkness into light. Into open air with savaged breath. This was magic. Out she popped. But she knew she needed to do more.

For women, love quelled so much. She knew that her voice could be turned to whispers, that her steps could lag behind the larger torso of the man, that magic meant give in to the superior will, the superior dream. And she knew that magic depended on faith. And dogged love like faith depended on magic.

Or a sleight of hand. His last trick. A card chosen from a shuffled deck. Then the magic. From his breast pocket he pulled out a photo of himself with the card in full view. She knew how he did it. The way he turned her to an image too, tight in his pocket.

At night she curled into him like a backwards c--wrestled with her own angels in her dreams. Drowning dreams. She lived his dives in the river, shackled, like her own body, drenched, then, saved. For isn't this what love bequeaths? Women can be drowned in love.

But not her. Not always. She wanted to step out of his shadow. Escape from the cards he dealt. Had to resist.

She had to devise her own magic despite his unfurling dreams. Unwind the thread of her own life. An endless blue ribbon twirled out of a black top hat.

She resisted erasure with her own kind of sassy grace.

The title is from a headline: "Resisting Erasure Through Grace" Mihee Kim-Kort, Sunday Review, New York Times, 3/28/2021—a form of a golden shovel prose poem.

CHAPTER 2

Memory: What We Know

Graceful Grit

Colleen Geraghty

In the moisture of seedtime,
in the squish, squishing sucking mud,
when the spring winds arrived igniting the legend
of my Irish grandfather
I hear his old brogue lilting
across memory's pond
and at the threshold of the garden, I see him
waiting for me. He is wild as old wood,
bent-backed, smelling of whiskey and sweat,
and he's kneeling,
yes, kneeling,
and he's kissing the ground.
His fingers dig deep into the earth's flesh,
crooked, arthritic hands cupping
the graceful grit into his palm.
He laughs aloud, makes the sign of the cross,
sprinkles dirt onto his tongue.
And yes, he swallows the gift.
While blades of croci, tender shoots of daffodil,
sleepy-eyed and bleary, struggle
to resurrect bud and bloom,
my Irish grandfather stoops to the earth,
smitten with the wild, fragrant blush of earth blossoming.
A long journey back from winter for some,
But not for him, my grandfather.
No, no, not for him.
At the blustery and uncertain cusp of spring
when winter fights the good fight, screeching
like a mourner holding on to grief,
my grandfather genuflects
in the garden, swallowing the graceful grit of earth.

Among the Heliotrope and Roses
Tana Miller

my baby sister and I   she's seventy-three
sit in my garden   reminiscing
childhood's memories spill from our tongues
some so sweet we hug ourselves   others
shards with sharp edges

mama was a slapper

my sister recounts the last time
mama slapped her face
sister slapped her back
mama slapped her other cheek   harder
sister slapped mama again
they stared at one another   cheeks scarlet
tears rise in sister's eyes
how could I have done that? she whispers
I pat her arm   remembering
when mama last slapped my own face   I was twenty-two
jiggling my baby in my arms
had done a load of his clothes in her washer
I had used too much laundry detergent she said
did I think she was made of money?
and why did I assume I could waltz in and do my laundry at her house?
I never loved mama after that   not really
my sister and I clasp our hands together   squeeze hard
safe now   cozy as two old bugs in a rug
ancient sinners weeping a little
among the heliotrope and early roses

Wednesday's Child

Kappa Waugh

Let me tell you how alluring Mr. Slauson's paint shack was to a seven year-old. It was kid-sized, six feet wide by eight feet, with a door, and a shed roof. The appeal increased by its being usually padlocked. The inside smelled of oil paint, turpentine, linseed oil, which prickled in the nose. The shack was painted white, inside and out, and sat ten feet from our back door. Since we lived in college housing, our yard was not really ours. We could plant some vegetables in it. The college had built a small playground for faculty children, and there was Mr. Slauson's shack.

He seemed old to me then, but Mr. Slauson was probably in his forties, dressed in a white tee shirt and white painter's overalls in the summer. Fall and spring the shirt was long sleeved in that mild, Virginia weather. Winters he didn't paint much but made repairs elsewhere around the college. He had let me in the shack a few times, and I could see it would be just perfect, for what nineteen fifties kid did not need a fort, a clubhouse, a hideout, a place where parents couldn't find you, a place to escape from siblings. It contained paint cans with wire handles, canvas drop cloths, painting rags, and brushes. One small window with three dusty panes and one broken, empty one, plus the white items inside kept it from being too dark, just dark enough to add to the allure.

On the times I found it unlocked, I went in and took possession. A few paint cans rearranged made table and chairs on a rug of drop cloth. When Mr. Slauson caught me at it, he didn't seem to mind. "Put them paint cans back against the wall. Fold up that drop, and skedaddle." Another time, closer to dusk when he found me inside, it was, "You can bring a flashlight in, but don't you bring no candle or matches. Them fumes could light up and blow you clear to kingdom come."

The day I want to tell you about was hot and sticky. I checked the padlock and saw the little bit of space on the bolt that meant the owner wanted to make it look locked, without actually locking it. So in I went. When I heaved some paint cans around to make my usual furniture, I discovered a new element in my hideout. There, against the wall lay a thin bundle, wrapped in mottled, red newspaper, about three feet long.

As I squatted down to unwrap it, a metallic odor, copper or iron, began to mix with the sharp paint smell. I pulled apart the layers of paper, meeting some resistance at the end. Blood, hair, bone, gristle and a sweet, rotten stench filled the air. My gorge rose, but I swallowed it back down. I had uncovered four long, thin legs, ending in little black hoofs-- deer I thought. What did this mean? Who would cut the legs off a deer, much less wrap and stow them in my hideout? And why? The room darkened.

"Well I see you found my package, Miss Curiosity-Killed-the-Cat. What do you think of my little deer-pretties?" I whirled around from my hunker, falling on my backside.

"No, don't get up; I like seeing you that way." I crab-scrabbled backward and fetched up against paint cans as Mr. Slauson advanced. You got pink panties on, like another little gal I knowed. Do yours have a day on them, like Wednesday?"

He knelt down next to me, and I just got overwhelmed. The heat, the smells, my discovery, Mr. Slauson's new, and much too personal tone, all worked together to make me sick. Spit suddenly flooded my mouth, and I vomited all over his white overalls. He reeled backwards as I jumped up, and ran out. Standing by the door, I called in, "I'm so sorry Mr. Slauson. I didn't mean to upchuck on you. Please don't tell my parents." "I won't tell them if you won't," was his reply. I went inside to drink Kool-aid and wash away the sour taste in my mouth. But each time I thought of those deer legs, I shivered and smelled them again. I kept sniffing my fingers, convinced they reeked of blood and vomit, even though I had washed my hands with black lava soap twice. My perfect hideout was no longer my special place. I got a book, but I couldn't settle to reading. I sat on the screened porch, going over the time in the shack, watching for Mr. Slauson to leave. He finally did, but this time he carried the long bundle that must be those deer legs, now wrapped in a canvas drop cloth.

After waiting a long time to make sure he wouldn't return, I got a box of matches from the kitchen everything drawer and went out back. Sure enough, the shack door was locked. I lit a match and pushed it between the door and the jamb. It burnt out. I went around

to the window, lit another match, and dropped it through the empty pane. Nothing happened. I couldn't stop thinking about those deer legs. After lighting a few more matches with no result, I lit the whole box and pushed it through the window. This time there was a WHOOMP, and the fire caught hold. I ran next door to the Western Union Office, burst in the door and yelled, "FIRE! Mr. Slauson's
paint shack is on fire!"

The fire engine came quickly, but the shack burnt down to the ground. All the grown-ups kept explaining to each other and to the kids who gathered to watch, how oily rags can spontaneously combust from the fumes, and how the paint in the cans would speed up the blaze. The college may have built Mr. Slauson a new paint shack, but it wasn't in our back yard.

My Long-Lost Friend Remembers Nothing Now
Mary K O'Melveny

I.

For more than forty years, our lives tracked every heartbeat: each lost
and found love, each good book, bad joke, glass of wine, holiday meal,
hospital visit, first sentence on a blank page. Each major and minor
key of our lives became as treasured as a Haydn symphony. After her
son died, she turned to gardens to transform her life, as tiny seedlings
became floating rainbows. These days, at any moment, I am still startled
by sights of flower beds awash in lilacs, lavender, lobelia, Queen Anne's
lace. I expect to see her there, smiling, as if she had just settled each
tender bloom into the earth. I can hear my name as she calls out to me.

II.

Where do memories go when no one is able to recall them? Each
communion circle emerging like skipped rocks on water: prickly family
gatherings, nights of passion or dissapointment, teardrops shed as a lover
left us or a child emerged to greet solid ground. Each intake of breath as
a world transmuted to orange, scarlet, mauve at sundown, each skein of
skin turned to rhinestone glitter beneath a thunderous rainstorm. Each
finely twined life tightly woven like a Gee's Bend quilt from scraps of
uncertainty, ribbons of bewilderment, thinned fabrics of hope and loss.

III.

I try to Imagine missing memories as prayers whispered in shadowed
night like Scheherazade's life-saving verses. Or a murmuration of
starlings as they scatter wide to whirl, frenzied for an instant before
they settle anew beneath a boreal sky. Maybe they are nascent notes
contemplated by songbirds while they shelter from passing rainstorms.

Or psychedelic colored mandarin fish radiating like geisha fans between coral reefs. Or perhaps they reside in simple buds emerging from June's earth, whose full blossoms will today catch the eye of a stranger, make her stop and think again about stories that once moved her to the brink of love.

We Gather It All In
Jan Zlotnik Schmidt

A bronzed curled copper beech leaf
A fly a moth caught in a spider web
A shriveled quince
A rotted pine green shingle
A dried bird's nest
one cracked robin's egg still there

A frayed white paper doily
A crystal cake plate
A silver candy dish
A tarnished thimble
An embroidered linen tablecloth
yellowed with age.

Rubber stockings
A rumpled housedress
A wooden chopping bowl
with a residue of grease
Recipes for lime Jell-O mold
stuffed cabbage
written in a mother's hand

A father's spectacles
His Fossil watch with an alligator band
Drafts of his poems in a crimped script
Journals with half done haikus
an empty one with white birch on the cover

A child's molar left in an egg cup
A pair of size 3 Nike sneakers on a bookshelf
A broken Slinky and Etch a Sketch
Masters of the Universe and
a Fisher Price Garage

Letters from a war long ago
in an illegible hand
stuffed in a plastic bag
Daybooks
white blank pages
stacked on a shelf
All in the wake of longing

Merry Goddamn Christmas
Kit Goldpaugh

"And that," I tell my visually and auditorily impaired Shih-Tzu, Uncle
Buzz, "is how Aunt Michele and I learned our Christmas carols." Uncle
Buzz and I are on route to PetSmart for his holiday grooming. I'll
request red hair bows with tiny bells. I don't mind humiliating Buzz in
the least. The little dingo wannabe has bitten me for eleven years every
time that I have cleaned the schmutz from his runny eyes or attempted
any nail or other personal care. Maybe I'll ask the groomer to paint
Uncle Buzz's nails red. For Christmas.

Buzz and I are listening to 92.1 FM and singing along with Bing
Crosby and Burl Ives. I tell him that I learned all these songs from
Mr. Doyle's Christmas choir of angels when I was a little girl. Mr.
Doyle lived across the street from us and was, among other things,
an electrician. He was an alcoholic, too. Every year on the day after
Thanksgiving, tipsy Mr. Doyle climbed to the top of his house and strung
lights around every corner, gutter, window, drainpipe and door. On the
roof sat a life size, fully loaded and ready for take-off sleigh and eight
huge reindeer. Santa waved from his seat. On the lower roof, over the
front porch, stood a choir of plastic angels, eyes closed, mouths and song
books open. A record player piped music through huge speakers secured
to the house directly behind the angels. A star was suspended from the
porch. Down on the lawn stood a family of snow men in various festive
poses, and across from them stood the Nativity scene: Holy Family,
manger, livestock and visiting royalty included. Every inch of every
figure from Rudolph's nose to the third king's box of myrrh was made
of plastic and every inch glowed like Hiroshima. Every time that Mr.
Doyle hammered a nail or moved a light, he bellowed, "Merry Goddamn
Christmas." He said it all day.

In the early 1960s, outrageous light displays were reserved for store
windows and Disneyland, but because of Mr. Doyle, our street was a
show-stopper. It took him all day. When he finally turned the lights
and music on, it was a beautiful thing. Half the street was as bright as
day. "Tasteless, obscene," proclaimed my mother. "You'd think they were
Italian."

"Oh, look!" said my sister Michelle, "There are penguins this year!"

"For Christ's sake," muttered my mother lighting a cigarette.

"Somebody has to pay for all that juice," said Dad.

"Mr. Doyle's an electrician. He gets all that stuff for free," Michelle assured our father.

"Lucky Bill Doyle," said Dad walking out the door.

"Merry goddamn Christmas," cried Mr. Doyle above the choir of angels.

"Merry goddamn Christmas," muttered Dad.

Every night at dusk from Black Friday into January, Doyle's house sang joy to the world. The lights went on, and the traffic picked up. Drivers involuntarily swerved toward the display, hitting other motorists doing the same. From our bedroom on the third floor, even the accidents were exciting, bringing police cars and more lights and lots of new swear words. Mr. Doyle gladly offered to explain details of the accidents to the police. So many lights! It was the most wonderful season of all.

The nightly caroling helped us maintain our holiday spirit for the entire season. We opened our windows unnecessarily wide to hear the plastic carolers better. There were bars on our windows so that we wouldn't fall to our untimely deaths in Mr. White's driveway because Mrs. White would have made us clean up our own broken body parts, Christmas or not. The Whites hated us, but we had to be polite and exercise company holiday behavior. When we greeted them, we wished them a merry goddamn Christmas.

My family was not destitute, but neither were we middle class like the lucky kids whose fathers worked for I.B.M. We were a few rungs above the Cratchits. Our parents' employers provided heat and health insurance, which was good, even though nobody was crippled or on borrowed time. Like the Cratchit girls, our hand-me-down dresses were "brave in ribbon," but unlike the Cratchits, we had TV. We watched all the specials: "Frosty," "Rudolph the Red-Nosed Reindeer," "Amahl and the Night Visitors," and my/our favorite, "Mr. Magoo's Christmas Carol." Those poor misfit toys! Poor Rudolph! Poor Tim Cratchit! Through the miracle of television, we learned to be grateful and generous and humble and joyful, virtues that we practiced from Black Friday to the Feast of the Epiphany.

Every Christmas Eve, while the plastic angels announced the arrival of the Christ Child and Santa, Santa himself strolled up and down the street, ringing a big bell in one hand and sipping a highball in the other, calling, "Ho Ho Ho." Santa had a very red nose that looked just like Rudolph's, but with more broken capillaries, like Mr. Doyle's, and the new Santa standing outside of PetSmart today.

Uncle Buzz and I head into the grooming salon. I say, "So you see, Uncle Buzz, it was Mr. Doyle who taught our whole neighborhood to sing and swear with holiday glee." Uncle Buzz growls, dog-speak for merry goddamn Christmas.

Alabama Summer 1949

Tana Miller

I half-skip across the cemetery
between my grandparents
my taciturn granddaddy
is dressed head-to-toe in tan work clothes
granny's hatchet-face is rigid
we walk as the crow flies between headstones
step directly on flat rectangles
marked: MOTHER   BABY   WIFE
the hot air is as still   as jittery
as the death around us
I am sweaty/out-of-sorts
we pause at the hand pump
after granny fills her two buckets
they allow me to lean into the icy water
and drink my fill   a delicious cold stream
drips down my chin
we walk until we reach a speckled-marble headstone
granny waters the azalea bush
helps granddaddy pull weeds for a bit
then she stands stone-still   her back to us
I trace the name BOBBIE ANN MITCHELL
engraved on the stone   close my eyes
try to picture the aunt   dead years and years before I was born
family legend/three-year-old paragon of beauty and sweetness
trapped alone under this brown parched ground
sticky cold creeps up my bare legs
trickles into my heart
my eyes open   granny is leaning down
close to me   I study the face powder stuck
in the lines crisscrossing her face
it was Jesus   she whispers   *Jesus wanted Bobbie Ann with him*
we three sad & silent souls
begin the march of the living
back toward granddaddy's dusty black Ford

In the life I didn't lead, I killed him

Colleen Geraghty

One sunny Tuesday, him out on the stoop smoking,
half-in-the-bag and black with the whiskey,
an eye like a stinkin' eel,
I snuck up behind him, flung a bicycle chain around his fleshy neck,
pulled as hard as I could.

In the life I didn't lead, I killed him.

My foot swung swift and sure, I struck him
right between his drunken shoulder blades,
him slumping forward like Santa's full sack.
Him gasping for breath, hot spittle choking the night air
like slick rain.

In the life I didn't lead, I killed him.

Choke-chain ruptured a pulpy vein,
tore an artery. His pickled eyes bulged frantic,
his blue lips whistled death's rattling rail
and his son-of-a-bitch, lying-tongue
blackened like a mission fig in summer's belting heat.

It was harvest time that Tuesday,
my fed-up, had-enough foot thrust deep
into his inebriated back
broke the cage where his heart
should have been.

In the life I didn't lead, I killed him.

I dumped his body in the Susquehanna River,
let her have her watery way with him,
like he'd had his way with me. She sucked him below
the strainers – rough waves and river stones battering him,
wasting his pink freckled flesh, bloating his body blue.
In the life I didn't lead, I killed him.

Yeah, I killed him, and after I'd thrown his life's carcass
into that old river, I built a fire from driftwood and dross.
I lay down in the mud, watching the blue-red flames
flick and fly into the night sky, the river growling
her tough-love lullaby,

Far away now from the life he'd choked out of me,
the hell-hole he'd built from whiskey-stoops
and finger fucks, I floated, heaven bound,
and peaceful because, in the life I didn't lead,
I'd killed him.

Joseph Cornell and Houdini

Jan Zlotnik Schmidt

*(Joseph Cornell watched Houdini perform at
Coney Island in 1905 when he was a young boy.)*

Boxed-in worlds.
Boxes that trap memory.
Boxes that enclose and hold in desire.

A miniature woman, looking like Frieda Kahlo,
is suspended in her shallow wooden box.
Held up by threads, filaments attached
to a firmament in wood.
Perched in air, her blue cobalt
flowered skirt fanned out like a tiny
parasol, she hangs there paralyzed
in her etherized world.
Waiting to be set free. Or maybe not.
Maybe she's caught in a moment of desire.

In another box of his, the firmament is dreamed
black with specks of stars, a petrified cosmos.
Constellations, like flecks of white dust.
Orion, Ursa Major, Cassiopeia, the North Star
in a spangling of hope. And in the front of the box,
fluted large emptied wine glasses speak
of once human presence. A couple, perhaps,
staring out at the night sky. Remembering their youth.
Their desire to break free. Their unfettered longing.

Did the young boy who watched Houdini
swathed in black cloth, then shut in a trunk
and finally emerge to gasping crowds,
imagine the lure of boxes trunks and closed in spaces?
What they could provide.
And did Houdini love that feeling of crouching
wreathed in chains, inside a trunk,

in utter darkness set down in the sea?
Hunched over, did he have the pleasure of
suspended motion, of hearing only his sharp intakes of breath?
Did time stop for an instant as he remembered
his surge to the surface of the sea
then the quiet return to dark depths?

Did they both crave these dark worlds?
That solitude, that silence,
that stillness of memory.

Memory Against Forgetting

Mary K O'Melveny

South Africa understood
our need for active memory.
At Liliesleaf, Mandela hid
until betrayal, trial, jail.
Now, liberation history
is spelled out along paths he walked
so people will always know how
to preserve their truest stories.

Here, in these un-United States,
the power of remembrance is in doubt.
Each day, falsehoods spill out like echoes.
Future chroniclers will no doubt be amazed
at the shadows cast by ghosted truths.
How we were asked to remember events
that did not take place. To unhear. To unsee.
Power's pronouncements shape-shifted daily.

We once believed in veracity, not false
versions of it. Our eyes were trusted guides.
Before too long, someone will design
a museum to enshrine not what was
but what was wished for. Authenticity
will be locked away, replaced by panoramic
pipe dreams, shiny trinkets that resemble
facts, alternatively remembered.

CHAPTER 3

Honoring Craft: From Villanelles to Golden Shovels

Acrostic: Bone House Redux
Eileen Howard

Bones, a compendium auricular,
Occipital heads the list.
Nasal turbinate breezes in, to
Endure the crush of a fist.

Here the plot thickens, as
One partial parietal devolves from the mist,
Under the rib cage hidden, by an aerialist.
Scandal, a murder, a shot back of the head.
Extreme trapeze skullduggery sans anesthetist.

Reordered phalanges make clear a mind depraved:
Especially confusing for a puzzled archeologist.
Devil take the tailbone. Bones' hearts safeguarded
Understood, within the
Xiphoid Process, with a loving kiss.

What Would Marcel Do?
Kappa Waugh

At the Marseilles railroad station,
by the shuttered snack bar
stand the vending machines.
Not so different from the U.S.,
filled with ranks of Mars Bars,
Kit Kats, potato chips and Cokes.
But then a hanging bag,
same garish colors as the others,
offers, of all things, madeleines.
What would Marcel do?
Would he fish in the pockets
of his white linen suit,
look with some perplexity at five
euros in his palm, deposit one?
Would he believe the pack's promise,
"made with fresh eggs," then push
the button for numéro trente-quatre?
Marcel regards the bag's advance,
its drop. He plucks it from the tray.
The shiny mylar sack may give him
pause. Will he use the pen knife
in his pocket? I can't think
he'd tear it open with his teeth.
The package broached, a sweet smell,
artificial vanilla rises. Does he
recall the scent of cheap perfume,
of overworked and under-washed servants?
Do station madeleines merit a taste,
a chapter, a century of memories?

My Grandmother's Cup

Colleen Geraghty

The sun yawns awake, casts her haughty gaze
over the black journals that fill my shelves,
dark books clumped together like lumps of coal
waiting for my hot fingers, for my word shovel,
for the tinderbox inside my tongue.

Though stories may gather like dust motes
on the cusp of the day,
sometimes I can't find my way
into the room where the words live,
so I wash the dishes instead.

I make beds, fold the laundry,
open yesterday's mail, pay some bills.
I tend to the plants.
When the words won't budge
I throw wood on the fire, set the kettle to boil,
wait for my morning tea.

Today, the big maple leans heavy into the cedars.
Last year's hurricane, a big whirling dervish, spun through my woods,
uprooted the heft of that tree. Now she bows and creaks,
moans like an old woman threatening to sink into the mud,
her summer bright leaves withered now,
scattering like embers in the cold wind.

While all my narratives lie sleeping like punished children,
morning rises in my mouth,
rolls around like yesterday's fire gone to ash,
the stormy path of what is no more smolders
in the furious cache of all my *shoulda, woulda couldas.*

I sit and stir honey into black tea,
lick the sweet nectar from the spoon,
marvel at the bees, their commitment
to the work, to the flowers, to the hive,
to their glorious Queen.

I sip tea from my grandmother's cup,
the one she'd pushed across the table towards me
before she died. The old cracked cup Aunt Sarah had swiped
from the kitchen of the big house, the last thing she took
before they'd turned her out.

White as a boiled egg, my grandmother's cup,
simple and startling,
snowy as a winter field at dawn,
like the empty pages
in the black-bound journal in my lap.

I wait and watch, sip my tea,
listening to the maple groan in thick wind.
I lick the honey from my fingers. I pick up the pen.
Like a river committing to a mountain, carving
herself a path to the sea,

like the bees giving it all up for the flowers, or the midnight sky
spitting stars for a child to wish upon,
I spill a torrent of waiting words onto the page—
I empty my cup,
rise, give myself to another day.

Villanelle for a Grieving Mother
Mary K O'Melveny

She sought refuge with a desperate thirst.
Unquenched, it sent her to our border.
How would she know her heart could burst?

Perhaps some readers are unversed:
Imagine leaving all behind in order
to seek refuge? With a desperate thirst,

those in greatest need leap headfirst.
Their desolation defeats any warder.
How could she know her heart would burst?

She carried her children with her. At worst,
she believed in salvation's ardor.
She sought refuge with a desperate thirst.

Belief in miracles was what she nursed
as they crawled through deserts. Hope's hoarder,
how would she know her heart would burst?

Now, she's jailed, her children all dispersed.
Any moment, alone, they will deport her.
She sought refuge with a desperate thirst
and now she knows. Her heart will burst.

Medea's Mother's Day
Tana Miller

I sing nursery rhymes through the wild night
while my lion's teeth hack fur fat flesh bone
blood like hard rain blesses Hecate's rite
the dead   the half-dead   glisten in the slight light
gruff goats   blind mice   gurgle and groan
I sing nursery rhymes through the wild night
the farmer's brave horse puts up a fight
I snap my fingers and turn him to stone
blood like hard rain blesses Hecate's rite
Mary's meek little lamb   so pure   so white
dies with three gored pigs by the old millstone
I sing nursery rhymes through the wild night
my blameless babes tremble with fear and fright
to see the horror their own mother has sown
blood like hard rain blesses Hecate's rite
I love you I screech   raise my knife and smite
my children   their father's sin to atone
I sing nursery rhymes through the wild night
blood like hard rain blesses Hecate's rite

About Milton Avery's "Girl Writing": The Phillips Collection
Jan Zlotnik Schmidt

> *"An image pierces the memory and bounces off an answering memory from the past."*
> *Joni Tevis, "The Wet Collection"*

On a still gray January morning
I gaze at her   at her white dress
page boy and curled bangs
I stare at her back   she leans away from me
her face her features unknown

Bent over a writing desk
a plank of slanted oak
she tilts her head downward
Her fingers curled around a pen
A page half-covered with an indecipherable script

The image pierces memory
Another teenaged girl peers out
 a bleak winter morning
 a catalpa tree   its branches once loaded
 with slimy mahogany pods now bare dusted with snow

I wonder about the
words written on the page
invisible messages
I imagine the flow and lilt of language
like the tilt of a swallow's wing

So unlike the girl's tensed body at night
bitten fingernails arched back
itchy flesh as she contemplates
what to confess on the page
what her parents can't know

I look again at the figure in the painting
Her white dress flows over her
thin limbs   she is poised to write
dreams or nightmares   it doesn't matter

Then I notice the dress is not all white
Flecks of red embroidery dot the
puffed sleeves   ice blue
pleats streak down the cloth
like rivulets in a half-frozen stream

Golden Shovels*
Eileen Howard

From "A Sunset of the City" by Gwendolyn Brooks

The night's alight with moonshine. **Come:**
keep pace with me, though you're not **there.**
As memory snuffs out, never-the-less, we **shall**
touch each other's hearts. For a second **be**
once more intact. Once there was **such**
balancing closeness. But tides are **islanding**
us in our marbled pasts, now separated **from**
each other. Alone. Each facing our unique **grief.**

Locked in her room, Harriet at 88, opened a **tin**
of beans. Her wild youth provided no **intimation**
of the constriction and constant isolation **of**
her later years, when a chocolate mousse or **a**
spell of sitting on her porch in evening's **quiet**
or a finch at her feeder would please her to her **core.**
Her wish: for all her past devastations finally **to**
fade. That silence and firelight would let her **be.**
For me, may a night of thunder, wind and rain fade **my**
indentured time in the bleakness of the **desert**
of lost joy, lost love, lost dreams, lost hope **and**
lost essence, and, I hope, evanesce, taking **my**
torment away for all time, leaving only **dear**
memories as my companions and my soul's **relief.**

A Golden Shovel is a poetic form which uses another piece of writing (or any part of the writing) and creates a new work using each word of the original as the last word, in order, of each line of the new piece. Read down the last words in these examples to discover the original piece.

Dig Out with A Golden Shovel
Tana Miller

1. The Hook

beckoned from the bed I had crafted from sticks by **the**
Feminist Sisterhood Choir   attired in work boots singing **mysterious**
songs about The Promised Land & the strength of **alchemy**
to change dirt into a womyn-owned wonder-world **of**
communes/child care they projected portraits & **images**
of Betty Friedan on my wall I kissed my refrigerator goodbye **&**
marched out the door in a velvet quilt sewn of birdsong's **words**

New York Times, Jillian Steinhauer, Instagram Now, March 31, 2021

2. The 20th Century Escape Caper

chop the century in half   out I creep to spend **many**
days (despite brain power loving heart) as charmbermaids **many**
more as laundress sex worker chauffer babysitter grounds' keeper   **hours**
days months years morph into a swarm of cawing ravens **&**
I fight to escape their claws until the radical wind **that's**
feminism sweeps the air clean   blows through tract houses pisses off **my**
husband   &   as I run for the door   I remember my **purse**

New York Times, Margaret Lyons, "King of the Hill," April 1, 2021

CHAPTER 4

Mythology and Spirituality: Known and Unknown Gods

The Scent of Zachariah
Kappa Waugh

Some priests' wives
welcome the men
home to their reek
of blood, but mine
enters wreathed in
incense. The words redolent,
mantled, suffused, lie
in my mouth like honey.
His hair, his beard, his
shawl, his very skin
was steeped in incense.
I longed to drink him in,
to drain him, drowning
in his sweet scent, but
our drinking days were
long gone by. He was old,
I was barren. Those dry,
unperfumed words said all
our was and is and is to be.

But then, a month ago,
he rushed in, speechless,
led me to our bed, and
made a fragrant oasis
for us both.
My expected roses have
not bloomed this month,
for hope has taken root.
My muted husband cannot say
his temple prayers, so has not
gone to work, yet our small house
still smells of frankincense.

One More Snake
Tana Miller

Pallas   not interested
    dry as salt   was accosted
by lust-driven Hephaestus
    within those oft-fraught Greek woods
 her struggle   no matter how sincere
    amplified his fire
    caused him to spew his stream upon her thigh
the disgusted virgin flung his spray into the dirt
where: molded from semen slick mud
    the seed grew from blind fish to mewling male-child
Erichthonious   miracle babe
    born without a mother's sheltering womb
    product of errant semen-spattered dirt
firm-lipped-tight-hipped   heartless Pallas
placed whimpering Erichthonious
    snake-ugly   unsuckled   unloved
within a wicker box   locked the box with leather straps
thrust the box toward Cecrop's three unmarried daughters
    Pandrosos   Herse   foolish Aglauros
never never look within the box   the goddess hissed
despite what she had been told   the third daughter opened the box
unleashed the motherless snake-child upon the world
nothing is surprising here   it is an old stale tale
    sperm are always marching   climbing thighs
    fighting through jungles   swimming through dangerous swamps
    plotting to outsmart the rest of us
even Pallas   bearer of the giant virgin flag
    her nether parts under lock-and-key
had to deal with the squalling product of mud and stickum
does that seem fair to you?

Hail Mary in the Bathroom

Colleen Geraghty

I heard you say
HAIL MARY
I saw you kneel
FULL OF GRACE
before the sink
THE LORD IS WITH THEE
let the water run
BLESSED ART THOU
Mother
AMONGST WOMEN
I saw you wash
AND BLESSED IS
your weary face
THE FRUIT OF THY WOMB
I watched you kneel
JESUS
I heard you whisper
HOLY MARY MOTHER OF GOD
PRAY FOR US SINNERS
I watched you bow your head
and cry
Mary Queen of Heaven
my hope and comfort
source of grace
deliver me from the pains of hell
NOW AND AT THE HOUR OF OUR DEATH
AMEN
I watched you rise,
saw the lights go out,
felt your ghostly foot-falls
through night's bleak corridors
disappearing into sleep.

The Reincarnation Highway*
Jan Zlotnik Schmidt

Are you unaccountably a thinker, doer, a sorcerer, talker, wanderer,
vandal? Peacemaker, Beauty, Warrior? Are you saintly, vengeful,
notorious, compassionate? Do you know the roots of your being?

Are you mild-mannered not fractious, calm and collected, good-
humored not spiteful, hot-headed, or icy? And feelings come over you in
an instant...mysterious, awkward, and unknown.
Are you a Jack-of-All-Trades? A Worker? A hands-on guy? A numbers
person? Are you inventive? Strategic? Scheming? Sleazy? Undeniably
lazy? Do you bite your nails down to the nub? Do you procrastinate?
Do you hoard stacks and stacks of newspapers, compulsively—you can't
stop. Who were you? Are you?

Do you have a good lineage?

Seven eight decades are just not enough. Take the reincarnation
highway. Have you ever wondered why you fear heights, snakes, spiders,
water birds, or the color red?. Do you gaze in the eye of a stranger and
know her. Or do you have that old familiar feeling when you walk down
the crooked streets of old Quebec? Or anxiety attacks at the Parthenon—
perhaps you were slaughtered in ancient Greece.

You were always a man or always a woman, but maybe not. You
could have been a man or a woman, a spirit, a viper, hound, gazelle, or
fish. And your caring golden doodle is on the way to being a Buddhist
monk. It's all in the cycle.

Do you have mysterious pains and cramps, a birthmark like a
Rorschach blotch in the middle of your chest--like a shotgun blast--like
a boy killed on a battlefield centuries before? You have lived before and
will live again. Nine times dying. Nine times living.

You were a murdered soul, an assassin, a German villager, a bishop,
abbot, a rabbi, cavalry officer, alien abductee, a young girl in a
Polish ghetto, a courtesan in a Paris café, turn of the century, sipping
absinthe, a pioneer woman living in a cabin near the edge of a wood.

Always alternate stories. Who are you, who were you? Regression.
Karmic Cycles, Hypnosis, Trauma, Depression, Resurfacing, Healing.
Tarot, Psychic Readings, Natal Charts, Numerology.

Seven times dying. Seven times living. Fall into the light.

Go down the reincarnation highway. Strategies for a muted life.

A found poem, inspired and derived from a Google search.

Ibis Now Ibis Forever
Tana Miller

ancient Egyptians quaked at the stability of the natural world
respected beasts' otherness by preparing them for the after-life
stowed away great hordes of mummified cats jackals lions birds
generation-after-generation-after-generation
same bodies   same feathers   same roars/howls/songs
gods entwined with beasts/birds as helpmates   bedmates
Hathor-heavenly cow gifted milk from her white udders
to flood the Nile   each year re-created fertile Egypt
Anabis-Jackal sent sinners straight to the crocodile's belly
the better behaved to a perfect-Egyptian heaven

all well-and-good
but not for me

no dull repeating pattern for my children or their offspring
I cherish two grandchildren's Asian features
my great-granddaughter's hair cloud
as it floats above her light chocolate self
it is rebels I admire: the nectarine   the Anjou pear
the shape-shifting squash changing from fruit to vegetable
the rose that reverts to rogue-red
the mythical albino stag   I cherish
my own chance to jump over cracks
to travel far from the deep ancestral faults
I don't want mother's green eyes in my mirror
no matter how beautiful or creative she was
I don't want my grandfather's pursed lips pasted over
my grandchildren's sweetmeat mouths
choking life from their words

God Has a Zillion Refrigerators

Kappa Waugh

God has a zillion refrigerators, and
I am one. Inside find hot sauce of anger,
frozen chicken hearts. Open my door to see
baked goods, baked bads, half-baked ideas.
Stand before me, God, like a teenage boy,
staring till you find my two percent, and
drink me straight from the carton. Towards
the back, find containers of curdled hopes,
long past their expiration dates. Bend
before me, God, a small girl searching,
searching for the pearl of last night's tapioca.
In my crisper, most has gone soft and limp,
though some cilantro still puts forth new leaf.
Kneel before me, God, housewife of my soul:
wipe away the sticky bits, the spills, the spots.
Clean up the fruits, unused, dry, decaying.
Open my door, God, and let my light come on.

Artemis on a Wild Hunt
Mary K O'Melveny

> *"The night sky is a wolf's mouth today and Artemis, bathed in*
> *solitude, is on her wild hunt."* Nikita Gill

Finally, NASA may send a woman
to the moon. Artemis will carry new
explorers in search of life sources
that may have been missed by Armstrong, Aldrin,
Collins or those who followed along for a
few years until we decided there was
nothing much to see beyond some dusty
boot prints and a hastily planted flag.

Artemis, daughter of Zeus and Leto,
sister of Apollo, must have laughed out loud
when all the men piled into her brother's
namesake voyager. She is, after all,
goddess of the Moon, the hunt,
all that is wild and unknown. He,
god of poetry, song and dance, far better
suited to calming earthly unease.

What might Artemis be seeking on
hidden icy corners of the Moon's south
pole, concealed from our earthly point of view?
Its crepuscular surface is tightly sheathed,
almost virginal. Maybe that's the point.
Unspoiled. Unseen. Untouched. Not like
our burning, drowning planet, soiled from end
to end. Innocence long lost. Permanence in doubt.

There are no stags, hawks, boars or hunting dogs
to be unearthed on lunar soil. Soon they may
no longer be birthed on earth. So, it must be
ice that Artemis will pursue on this
stygian surface. As fires consume us,
nothing short of glacial rescue will do.
She raises her golden bow. Her arrows
fly toward an umbra of waning light.

Fith-Fath ("fee-fi")*

Colleen Geraghty

In this room of my own, simple and small, I say a fith-fath for safety
and for time standing still. Truth-teller, soothsayer, virgin and temptress,
Great Mother, old hag, crone in my stew, restore the ancient landscape of
my splintered heart. Fire up the forge that takes no wood, pull the Holy
Ghost into the flames. Let Her shout the mighty war cries of women
scorned, words made flesh, visible in flames.

Summon Morrigan, Babh, Macha, and Anan. Washer women at the
ford, rise up in my throat, split my tongue with your trio of truth: Purity
of heart. Strength of limbs. Action to match my speech.

Give me the strength to weave again the legend of one mother's life!
In the race to save man from his shame and dishonor, she gives birth to
a blessed child, but this time, her other mouth opens wide, ruby lips and
tongue shouting Macha's wild curse: "Let all men of the cloth, all men of
justice for all, let these men suffer the pains of childbirth every time they
open their mouths to misogyny and mistake it for holiness."

Oh, warrior Queen of old, you are the fire that takes no wood. You
are the burning in my heart when I rise today with a million holy ghosts
in my mouth, a million fragrant tales, bloody coat hangers fluttering like
dark crows at the edge of my tongue.

I shout with the courage you gave me at birth: "Purity of heart,
strength of limbs, action to match my speech--holy trinity of thee, light
the hills of Kerry, the 'Paps of Anu,' the corridors of Congress with the
childbirth pangs you know."

Bless me, oh great warrior Queen, bless me, bless us all.

**Pronounced "fee-fi," a Celtic incantation that renders a person invisible.
It was used by hunters, warriors, and travelers.*

Sky Sailing
Tana Miller

I might have been the trout stream
daddy took me to one early spring
      water sparkling over speckled rocks
      thick with life
but I wasn't the quicksilver stream
I wasn't the life within the stream
I was the red-nosed child
perched on the stream's cold bank
      bone-lonely   while her Daddy fished
I might have been Leah
the woman Laban tricked Jacob into marrying
the wife he never loved
I wasn't Leah
I was another wife   unloved unloved
I might have been formed of velvet or silver
      treasured
      handed down generation-to-generation
      instead I am ordinary flesh bone blood gristle
      dust
I might have been a savant
multiplying faster than light
      causing orange red yellow blue digits
      to flash slash crash in the air
I might have been an aria
      bringing an audience to tears   causing them to cheer
      stamp their feet   beg for more
I might have been the thoughtful skin between your beloved eyes
      sacred space where the lion and the lamb
      cleave to one another
I might have been the air above a stormy sea
      a feral howl
I might have been the emptiness between the planets
      nothing
      nothing
I am none of those

I am more
I am the flickering Milky Way
       at night I spread my gauzy-white body
       over the night sky & sail & sail

CHAPTER 5

Tales of the Natural World

Earth Science
Kit Goldpaugh

In college, in need of one more science credit to graduate, I
enrolled in an earth science class entitled "Sea Myths, Monsters
and Mermaids." The syllabus promised to explore the Bermuda Triangle
(electromagnetic forces in the ocean, seaquakes), the Loch Ness Monster
(geology of gorges and deep lakes and a huge sea slug, trapped like a
carnival goldfish too big for its bowl), and Big Foot (drunk hunters), and,
well, mermaids. Manatees and sea cows were mistaken for Rubenesque
mermaids by near-sighted, vitamin-deprived, sex-starved sailors with
rickets and scurvy, who were too long at sea. I learned that real manatees
have been rounded up (?) and relocated to places in South America where
they ate the vegetation blocking dams. Eco win-win. That might very
well have been on the midterm.

One question that was on the midterm was "Define and explain
DSL." DSL is the deep scattering layer of the ocean. It is horizontal
band about 300 – 500 meters below the surface just swimming with
schools of fish and all sorts of marine life. So abundant is the marine
life there that it gives off sound waves which initially had made land
dwellers playing with sonar think that they'd found the bottom of the
ocean. There was never a question like "Explain the symbolism the little
mermaid's transformation from sea creature to silent woman and her
eventual dissolution into sea foam. What does this story say about the
role of Danish women in the early nineteenth century?" Just water and
rocks.

In answer to the DSL question, one student wrote, "DSL is
a reverse process anti-hallucinogenic drug that makes the user see
things as they are and fly right. Predictable effects include cutting hair,
wearing patriotic colors, praying, and following the law. All
users experience a narrowing of the mind which intensifies with each
use. Some habitual users will join religious cults." Dr. Kelly read the
answer aloud and gave the student full credit for having such a clever, if
wholly wrong, answer.

At least once a week, some future conspiracy theorist would bring evidence of a recent sighting of Yeti, Big Foot's frosty first cousin dwelling in the Himalayas, to refute Dr. Kelly's teachings. Alien intervention was a frequent theory of these future science teachers of Texas to explain everything from crop circles to pyramids. Of the Bermuda Triangle, they might demand, "What about the Andrea Doria Dr. Kelly? The table was set and food laid out when the rescuers found it. It was the same thing on the Mary Celeste!" Dr. Kelly might inquire the researcher's source. He might suggest that the Andrea Doria crashed in Nantucket Sound. He might ask how likely, even after an alien abduction, it would be for everything on a moving ship to be undisturbed after months of abandonment by their captain in a biosphere of turbulent water, sea birds and scavengers. Another skeptical student might just call out, "Well, what about all of those downed planes? I read that Amelia Earhart died in the Bermuda Triangle." On days like that, I wished that I'd brought popcorn for the whole class.

Sometimes now, I think that I recognize one of my old classmates being interviewed on Fox News after a natural disaster, say, a category four hurricane in Florida or an extra month of fire season in California. One science teacher from Iowa explained that the media has turned weather patterns into the global warming myth. "The weather has been changing for hundreds of years," Mr. Werner said. "The liberal media wants to turn it into a crisis." After a thoughtful pause, Mr. Werner suggested that it's probably to cover something up. "They're always hiding something from us," asserted Mr. Werner, without providing an antecedent for either pronoun.

Along comes COVID-19! Imagine how many scientifically informed theories Mr. Werner (and his online friends I suspect) has explored during his lockdown. Daily news briefings alone provided buckets of conspiracy chum for the real scientists like him.

My own scientifically informed friend has forwarded articles to me so that I would finally understand that this virus isn't nearly as bad as I, a product of the liberal media, wants us to believe.

Here's the gist: The lockdown caused more death than the virus itself when you include suicide and depression, cancer patients missing treatments. The mask doesn't do anything but make it hard to breathe. Have you ever had to go in a public bathroom wearing a mask? Nothing. It still smells. The death rate is grossly overreported. What about all the people who died of regular flu or pneumonia? If they had COVID too, the hospitals just counted COVID because they get more money from the government for COVID. If the person has a heart condition or weakened immune system and they die, the hospital blames COVID. They were sick in the first place, she tells me. (I don't correct her apparent misunderstanding of preexisting conditions, of cause and effect, of the virus.)

She said that the former president was right; the virus would virtually disappear in the warm weather. She texted me an article about the restorative properties of sunshine and fresh air on soldiers during the 1918 pandemic. I did not respond that while I'm all for a day at the beach, this time I'd prefer a vaccine. As soon as travel restrictions were lifted, my friend, the science teacher, returned to Florida where she is preparing to move permanently.

"Flying now has never been easier or cheaper," she tells me . Sure, she has to wear a mask on the plane, but virtually nobody wears masks in Florida. She texts me from a farmers' market. She warns me not to get the vaccine. "The government rushed the production and won't allow you to sue if something goes wrong. It hasn't been tested enough." I think but don't say that this time we didn't test it on chimpanzees, orphans, and prisoners, in that order, as we did with the polio vaccine. My friend says that people are having terrible side effects, seizures, and strokes. She was talking with a physician's assistant at the farmers' market. "These vaccines might have been made in China so China could test on us. Some of the vaccines give you the virus, some of them alter your DNA." (Gasp!) "Pretty soon, they'll all come from China." I think but I don't say, "I hope so." I haven't been to Canal Street in years, and I remember a teahouse on Mott Street that made bubble tea. I agree that she shouldn't get the vaccine. I think but I don't say, the vaccine might interact poorly with the buildup of DSL in your system.

In the Dead Month
Colleen Geraghty

Here I am digging a death ditch
with an antler,
flipping sandy loam and fool's gold
over my shoulder,
keeping the devil at bay.

Here I am with a bone-white antler
digging a death ditch
for a winter rabbit,
snowball pure and still as ice,
his morning cage empty of everything but straw.

Here I am ready, but where's the good spade when I need it?
The pitchfork? The hammer?
Nothing but an antler and
chipping away at earth's flesh like a baker
cutting into a crusty pie.

Joshua High Desert

Kappa Waugh

Joshua High Desert, where the trees
look like pictures Jesus drew in
kindergarten, spiky dry, the fronds
klack-klack in the wind. In this
peaceable kingdom, Scorpion lies
down with Rattlesnake and
Kangaroo rat, under spreading
Creosote. This scrappy bush may
live ten thousand years. Rocks
hew to one palette: rusty red,
dusty gray, and ochre. Lick one
and spit dries too fast to see
it shine. Here old gods reign
where rain falls rarely.

Hecate's Dancing
Colleen Geraghty

I believe the dead are dancing in the stubble corn,
out beyond the sticky threads that bind us to our suffering,
behind heaven's brightest stars,
before we were born, endless joy
swung heavy on the lilt
and uplift of reaper's grim unyielding scythe.

I believe in Hecate's gifts,
the cessation of sorrow when spirits go marching
through heaven's gate,
trumpets blaring, drums rolling,
a couple of loud guitars, some flutes,
singing banjos, fiddlers, and one great horn of plenty.

I believe in the footprints hidden in the mud,
under the tongue of time,
buried in muscle and bone,
the germinating voice of the Seanachí,
alchemy's dream—the beauty
that sorrow can bring.

Out beyond the grief's sticky threads,
knee deep in the stubble corn,
Hecate's dead are dancing
wild Irish reels and crazy jigs,
pounding the earth
with the eternal sound of joy.

The Ocean at the End of the Lane
Eileen Howard

can i drop in uninvited
will the welcoming arms
of an octopus bid me welcome
give me a tour of the
emerald green sea bed

will urchins yell friendly
insults will starfish stare
askance   will hermit crabs shy away
will adventure dance
on my wet locks

will the deep resonate with chorales
will coral sing
a sea song lullaby
can i immerse myself completely
will the ocean give me gills

can i swim throughout the
seaweed jungles   watch parrot fish flit
from trance to trance
can i lose myself forever here
can i surrender to a deep water dance

Journal Entry: Great Horned Owl
Mary K O'Melveny

Some say that a poem is never
just about its subject matter.
Metaphor matters as much as
lyrical style or creative rhyme.

I thought of that today as I peered
from my perch at the forest's edge.
My grey striped feathers, tinged with white,
ruffled by the sharp autumn breeze.

A fat squirrel hurried to hide
beside a slab of once glacial
granite that now punctuates clusters
of echinacea, lavender.

Normally I hunt as night drifts
over the meadow, slips onto
tree limbs like grey silken stockings.
But today, sunlight caught my gaze.

I could see into the windows
of the blue house where two women
have made their own roost. One of them
brings seeds and nuts out all winter.

She's searching for an audience.
Some nights my audiobiography
wakes her. I question everything.
Today, just as I landed on

a thick branch, intent on my hunt,
she caught my eye and smiled.
And we paused, like a brief inhale,
to take stock of lives of others.

But then, my lichen-laden limb
felt too constricting. Open sky
promised other viewpoints. Sometimes,
we glimpse as much as we need to know.

The New York Botanical Garden

Tana Miller

young carp   red-orange streaks
dart in twos threes
engineered mutations
meticulously manipulated play-pretties
circle round green lily pads
older fish   gold leaf and watercolor
yellow white silver   orange-spotted black-spotted
push one plump fish-shoulder then the other
through the pond water   create froth   furls   ripples
forever cruising
o-mouths stretched wide wide wide
o baby baby baby
o-o-o-o
ornaments for an emperor's amusement
fit for nothing more
not sadness   not joy   not love
nothing more

Hemiceratoides Hieroglyphica

Eileen Howard

A friend said to me
"There is a moth in
Madagascar that
sips the tears of birds.
You could create a poem
from that...."

It sounded magical.
I dreamed Fantasia
morphing shapes and
colors, saw the moths
as comforting angels.
Saw the flutter of their
enfolding wings,
their taking the burden of
the birds' sorrows, as
something to gladden the heart.

I turned to the internet
to learn more about
this amazing ritual.
Would that I had never
sought more knowledge!

Just as dust mites up close
are revealed as
prehistoric monsters
that revolt on sight,
so too these moths. Their
Proboscides are not
soft, feathery mouthparts,
but implements
of torture. These
Madagascan moths
sneak up to predate
the tears of sleeping birds.

Now, birds have two
eyelids that they close
when sleeping.

The proboscides of Madagascan
moths have lethal looking
hooks and barbs
like ancient harpoons
to drill through the birds'
tender eyelids.

Scientists speculate that the
moths might inject an anesthetic.
But, then, how do these birds awake?

I think I have
a different poem...

Star Factories
Mary K O'Melveny

> *The Orion Nebula (home to the constellation Orion's Belt), is one of the*
> *largest star-forming regions in the universe and the closest to earth. Its*
> *core contains exceptionally bright O-type stars which are the hottest and*
> *brightest of all the stars. The Nebula can sometimes be viewed with the*
> *naked eye in an extremely dark area free of outside light interference.*

There is big one near Orion's Belt.
Think of the scene as a kind of Sam's Club
spread out above us, its vast parking
lot waiting for new stars to arrive.
Or maybe an Amazon Fulfillment
Center, the search for bargains always on,
rewards awaiting the swiftest hunters.

To the naked eye, blurs of rose, mauve,
Robin's egg blue. With Hubble's aid,
one feels an urge to wrap up in soft clouds
of rainbow light, roll around amidst
curves and valleys backlit by pinpricks
of new stars forming every millisecond,
each shaped like a mouth opened in wonder.

Heat and light radiate from this nebula
like sparks from steel factory furnaces
whose glow we barely recall down here
on Earth where assembly lines no longer
produce much of use to anyone. As our days
pass, memories of creation fade. Our fortunes
are now forged by the thrill of forming stars.

CHAPTER 6

Pandemic Reflections and Reactions

Dreamers

Mary K O'Melveny

> *....if dreams die, life is a broken-winged bird....*
> Langston Hughes

More than nine hundred thousand dead.
The ground is littered with feathers.

A shot glass resting at bar's edge.
A Yankees cap nesting on a coat rack.

A stethoscope stashed in a pocket.
A cell phone encased in a plastic bag.

A dog-eared book of Whitman.
An underlined Introduction to Chemistry.

An unopened collection notice.
An email returned by the daemon mailer.

An I Heart Grandma sweatshirt.
A Best Dad Ever coffee mug.

A Social Studies teacher's manual.
A pair of yellow rubber cleaning gloves.

A thermoplastic blue construction hard hat.
An antique freshwater pearl necklace.

A citizenship exam study guide.
A valentine, unopened on an oak desk.

A well-worn red plaid wool flannel shirt.
A pair of lightly scuffed Air Jordans.

A half-used jar of Pond's cold cream.
A half-drunk bottle of Jack Daniels.
A blackthorn Shillelagh with a copper tip.

A sauce-stained white linen chef's apron.

A beige wool cardigan sweater with a missing button.
A black silk dress with spaghetti straps, unworn for years.

A spruce-topped Alhambra Flamenco guitar.
A synthetic leather black and white soccer ball.

A Navajo wedding basket.
A Kente cloth dashiki, size XXXL.

A just-opened jar of Vaseline.
A dusty bottle of Old Spice.

A DVD of *The Great American Songbook*.
A floral tin index box of family recipes.

A still-open checkerboard on a coffee table.
A slightly rusted set of garden tools by the steps.

A red and white cotton kaffiyeh.
A pair of 2.5 Readers with a tortoise shell frame.

A carved bamboo Quran holder.
A naugahyde *Book of Common Prayer*.

A sepia-tinted wedding photograph.
A bronzed baby shoe.

A vintage denim jacket with copper studs.
A paperback copy of *The Autobiography of Malcom X*.

An original vinyl recording of *Sketches of Spain*.
A St. Jude rosary made of turquoise beads, blessed by Pope Francis.

A bright blue six-foot nylon dog leash.
An empty white wire bird cage.

The Villain

Eileen Howard

Covid 19 deserves a villanelle:

smothers the news, saturates air waves,

sounds, sounds again its wicked knell.

Sleeping, it weaves a terror-stricken spell,

we see body bags, ventilators and too many graves.

Endemic, epidemic, it comes in swells,

crests, crashes, makes us all slaves.

Sounds, sounds again its wicked knell.

Stories great and small, our children we'll tell,

unmitigated disasters and epic saves:

Covid 19 deserves a villanelle.

Social distancing works, but people rebel,

fight over use of masks, act like arrant knaves.

Covid 19 sounds its wicked knell.

It spreads in jail cells, hotels, a fond farewell,

scientists still puzzled over how it behaves.

Covid 19 deserves a villanelle,

even as it sounds its wicked knell.

A Nobody (Thank You Emily Dickinson)
Tana Miller

as she lives through plague-days
quarantined from a dangerous world
her chapped hands flutter   her bare feet dance
she sorts her t-shirts   folds her white sheets
chops onions   celery   peels knobby carrots
shreds poached chicken breasts for soup
visits her garden   tastes damp spring earth
whispers her guilty pleasure in the hellebore's ear
removed at long long last from the otherly world
where a deadly virus rampages across oceans   mountains
she is sequestered at home   sterile   careful
news of illness   death reaches her in raspy whispers
her former life is shuttered   locked down   stilled
even god has disappeared
she invents her own rhythm   cadence   desires
composes 1800 poems   sews them into rose-scented packets
stows them in a bedroom drawer
she is a blessed nobody too
forever grateful

How To Avoid Unwanted Attachments

Mary K O'Melveny

> *In June, 2021, osteopathic practitioner Sherri Tenpenny, an anti-vaccination activist, urged a panel of Oho State legislators to pass a bill that would prevent businesses or schools from mandating COVID vaccines. According to Ms. Tenpenny, the coronavirus shots "interface" with cell towers and "magnetize" recipients, causing a wide variety of metal objects to stick to their skin.*

A doctor in Ohio has warned us
that Covid vaccines can harm us.
Her evidence is quite distressing,
even though some facts are missing.

If you've become too close to your toaster,
blame those vaccines. Fox News will host her
to explain these connections. Do not rely
on science or metal objects will fly.

When someone puts shots in our arms (or
elsewhere), it's likely some snake charmer
who is really just trying to sell us
on a Bill Gates plot. Those overzealous

lackeys who promise cures don't tell us
that chips and magnets will soon propel us
toward doom. After you have been pricked,
your tableware and frying pans will stick

to you like glue. If you are ill at ease
with walking around while spoons and keys
adhere to your body like ornaments,
then it's wise to avoid such experiments.

Before we're laden with metal fragments,
let us finally abandon our attachments
to fake news. It is better to be a skeptic
than be bewitched by government medics.

Who says Covid's so bad anyway?
Everyone has to depart earth someday.
Better to do so unapologetic,
instead of becoming way too magnetic.

Early Covid Days
Kit Goldpaugh

The professor wants to know if I think we will lose anyone we know
to Covid 19. Yes, I think. We are definitely going to lose friends. I'm
pretty sure we are going to die, too. I don't tell the professor that. I tell
the professor that as long as we stay inside sealed in trash bags, latex
oven mitts and ski masks, and wash our hands until they bleed, we'll be
fine. The professor wants to help. He wants to continue volunteering at
the food pantry until I sit on the steps and weep.
Please don't go, I ask. Then, please don't go. If you get sick, that's
another hospital bed that didn't need to be used. My son suggests that if
the professor insists on going, I should encourage him and then 1
lock all the doors.

We have our affairs in order, sort of.

Do you want to be intubated? I ask.

What, now? No, he says.

Do you know what that means, I ask.

What? Like CPR? Yeah, no I don't want that. Don't we
have our DNRs all set?

Yes, but there are sub-categories. CPR is the chest punch.
Intubation is the ventilator.

We'll be fine, he says.

In the early '80s, Raymond Briggs published a graphic novel entitled
When the Wind Blows. The story follows a little old couple in England
preparing for a nuclear holocaust. They follow the government brochure
to prepare. They lean doors and pillows
against a standing wall and crawl into their lean-to to wait it out.

They are supposed to stay for fourteen days until the radiation is all gone, and it's safe to come out. But they crawl out early because she refuses to follow the toileting suggestions. They follow the instructions exactly, right down to taping the glass on the window panes so the panes don't crack. The story follows the couple as they wait for the mail, the newspaper, the milk man. They develop terrific headaches, diarrhea, bruises, and bleeding gums. It rains, and they want to make tea. But there is no gas or electric, and they are both so so tired. They lie down on the couch and promise one another that the next day they can dust themselves off, tidy up, and things will be fine.

I've already told the boys to put my ashes and bits and pieces into Mugs-o-Mom or Cups-o-Kit. Most of my life I've shared a bed with a sister or spouse. Now I fear that I'll end up in the Saugerties Ice Skating rink with dozens of other bodies, and I'll share a mug for all eternity with a stranger. Mug-o–Mom-Plus or Cup-o-Kit-and-Friends.

I can't die until I finish caning the professor's grandfather's Lincoln rocking chair. Every day, I weave, find a mistake, and pull it out. I start that section again and again. Like Penelope, I have no intention of finishing until I see that ship on the horizon.

The news grows worse. There aren't enough masks, gloves, gowns, shields. There aren't enough medical personnel. We can't borrow from our international neighbors because they don't have supplies either. Anyone who can stay home is told to do so. People who must work are cheered and given free pizza but not medical insurance. At home, we wear masks and wash our hand raw. We are told to imagine that the virus is glitter, and everything is covered in spangles.

Washing the imaginary glitter from the potatoes one night, I think about the couple in the Briggs book who had no water to wash the radiation from their dishes. I think about the old couple on the Titanic who snuggled in their bed together as the boat sank. I imagine the professor and me drifting away on an ice floe. The professor asks if I think we'll be okay. Absolutely.

Pandemic Summer
Tana Miller

I was a March carpetbagger   regaling in Florida faux-summer

joyful among pelicans & manatees

until waves of Covid turned us all into Chicken Littles

desperately seeking an escape from paradise

home to snow again   a shrunken life   I scrubbed

tomatoes carrots celery   searched

the internet for disinfectant toilet paper

became familiar with people wearing masks

 that made them look like cartoon bandits

talked to disembodied zombie-heads via Zoom

& watched death tolls climb like evil aerialists

spring lived itself out   surprising only in its nonchalance

the grape hyacinths lined the bluestone walkway

disappearing as days grew warmer   promising to return next spring

would that I had such surety about my own time-line

even the sun was casual as it brought early summer heat with no concern

for dead bodies stacked in trucks outside hospitals

I dig overgrown Stella Dora lilies   replant their tattered babies

a spiral shell the size of my thumb-nail catches my eye

I swoop it into my hand *where did you come from?* I ask

trace its circular path with my eyes:

it's a tornado whirlwind

the symbol of birth-death-rebirth

a body oozes from the home it carries   more goop than flesh

a head pops up from the slobber   sports two hair-like

tentacles which explore up down everywhere   a single foot

allows it to hike my hand's crannies calluses   seep over muddy skin

without warning   the body vanishes into its home

& I am flooded with longing for a safe place

where I can   at least sometimes

also retreat from this imperiled world

r=C/2π

Eileen Howard

The minutes drip away
the hours slouch off to Bethlehem,
the days intertwine, interweave.
The months melt away, leaving
only an iridescent snail trail.

Land locked, house bound, drowning
in silence. How to talk to friends
the other side of Zoom/ Skype/ WhatsApp?
How to negotiate social distancing:
talking through muslin,
managing a new normal?

Should I brave crowded
aisles of a supermarket,
march down the one-way lanes
in my colorful mask, which drifts
down below my nose if I try to speak?

Will we need new skills:
number of people in group X 6 feet
equals the circumference of a social
distance circle. Now find the radius
of that circle and stake out your backyard jamboree.

Summer Light
Jan Zlotnik Schmidt

Summer light illumines a dark tunnel of memory, a time before.
An insistent ingathering of flashes of light on the river, glints of
copper wings, maple twists floating to the ground, sunlight dappling
oak leaves in late afternoon. This was the light before. When you could
count on wind drifting through branches and know it would rustle your
hair. Know you could walk close to a friend on a trail and murmur
about your lack of sleep, or the screeches and yelps of coyotes at night,
and not worry if your breath was caught up in hers, or if there were
droplets in the air like dust motes.

There was a kind of light that shaded your dreams, or streamed a
path on the sea. Or was like the spark of sunlight on a stone skipping
across a creek. It was a time when you could brush against lilacs and
smell their fulsome perfume without a sense of loss. Or when you could
look at azaleas in your yard, blooming magenta and white as they never
had before, and not see the irony. And you don't want to be contrary or
joyless, but the earth is tilting beneath your feet. You remember when
you were a child spinning an old globe with your father down in the
basement, in the dust, where you had deposited it because the light didn't
work anymore; the countries weren't illuminated. The pastel pink and
blue patches of continents and oceans, the boundaries between countries
almost had faded. There were names that have long disappeared:
Siam, Burma, The Belgian Congo, Yugoslavia. And those that have
remained, Morocco, Egypt. You spun the globe with him, as continents
twirled beneath your fingers, while he named countries, capitals, rivers,
mountain ranges. Some with weird words—like the Volga, the Caucuses
or Mandalay.
He mapped out a world for you. Each place an imaginative terrain.
A world now existing in darkness, covered in a film of forgotten time.

You think how spirited you were, how your thoughts could traverse
the globe. The world as you knew it spun and then stopped, stopped by
your pointed fingers. You had that power.

When you think now of that imaginative terrain, the spinning silver
thread of his stories, you realize your world was illuminated by words,
much like the way sunlight sharpens the greens on the meadow, or the
watery reflections of upside-down trees in the river's afternoon light.
And you wonder what will summer light illuminate in years to come.
What memories and stories will emerge? What words will blot out all
others?

You wish you still could flip on a switch and see land masses,
the oceans lit up from within. You wish the globe had never dimmed.
Summer light vanishing, distilled to a glimmer of longing.

Covert Covid
Eileen Howard

Have you noticed?
How pictures of
a vacation you took
less than a year ago
seem like an event
from a different century?

How what then seemed like
an enjoyable ramble,
now looks like the most
improbable joyous
fandango? Remember?

In the streets of downtown
Providence Rhode Island
we got hopelessly turned around
and thought it was a lark:
saw a friend's recent
book prominently displayed
in a bookshop window.
A serendipitous find.

Did my daughter and I
really decide, spur of the moment,
to visit Roger Williams Park Zoo?
Now you have to book in advance,
social distance, wear a mask.
Now I only see her via Skype.

At the zoo, I lost my lens cap while
watching the red panda's antics.
A zoo person fished it out of
the pile of leaves at the bottom
of a fenced enclosure with
giant tongs, laughing. Imagine.

A face. Right in front of you.
Laughing. No mask....

Then we headed out to explore
an abandoned lighthouse.
Dipped our toes in the ocean.
Watched seagulls dip and soar,
whitecaps pink up in the setting sun.

Do you also, sometimes,
feel like an abandoned lighthouse?
Moored in one place?
Slowly eroding,
slowly losing your light?

Life in the Moment

Tana Miller

this spring I watch with wild wild yearning
as a male wren once again appears on my porch
flings out old debris from the birdhouse
builds a new nest from twigs   dry grass
grey hair harvested from my brush   bright bits of yarn
tail cocked upward   blustering   his mating song trills his intent
Jenny soon appears   creates her grass cup over his nest
lays a string of pale speckled eggs   they co-parent
taking turns sitting on the nest   make a mighty racket
if we try to peek   yet disaster often prevails:
dead-babies   crushed shells   splayed on the porch floor
contents swept up   thrown away by us   ignored by them
frayed voyeurs/sentinels   we watch two cycles from eggs to fledglings
this eerie-Covid-summer
as they live the life they've always lived
free from:

         regret
         fear
         dread
         future plans
         futile hope

Almost There
Colleen Geraghty

Captured in black and white, you are forever seated in a classroom. There is a tear in the left corner of this 48-year-old photograph from 1974. You are nineteen years old and in a classroom in Barcelona. How you came to Spain, or why, is a mystery I cannot fathom.

There are twenty-one other students in the photograph with you. Seventeen young people are smiling; two boys are frowning. Two girls have their heads buried in open books. You are seated in the front row next to the girls, your legs splayed wide. Your cut-off dungarees reveal your muscular thighs, and a five-o'clock shadow darkens your freckled face. You are smiling.

This old photograph does not show that you were on fire when you were born, so much fire that a thatch of red hair lit your fontanelle, the place where God breathed flames into your blood.

Oh, my passionate, hot-blooded, blood-brother, you were alive then, so alive you sizzled through the world like a lit explosive. Perhaps if you had been more like Padre Pio and less like Lucifer the world might not have crushed you under its ugly boot, ground your hot embers to dust.

In 1974, even in black and white, you are volatile as a volcano, your fire erupting through the world. Big blazing brother, your light was so bright it blinded you.

And now, I am on my knees. I am on my seared knees, and I am scrubbing.

It's November 2020. It's sleeting. The streets are turning to ice. The world is up to her neck in an isolating, death-grip of a pandemic, and I am on my knees.

I am scrubbing your blood, your piss, your shit out of the tile floor, out of the grout, out of the wood trim, out of the bathroom rugs. All of your fire, your red, red, fire – now clotted and pooled like crushed red cherries. And brother, mark my words, I am not wearing gloves. I am not wearing the Covid-compliant-safety-suit suggested by the coroner.

I want my flesh to feel you, my hot-blooded, hot-headed, blowtorch of a brother. I want to find your ember, your lit-explosive life.

I want you to coagulate in my pores, seep into the crevices of my palms, bleed into my lifeline, blot out my own fingerprints.

I want us to become the children we were, so many years ago, before life pulverized us, before we were broken, crushed, chewed up, and spit out like the worthless pieces of shit we were expected to be.

I want to remember you blossoming and fragrant as a fiery rose, your ragged thorns blistering through your blood, piercing the world.

In 1974, a photo captured you in black and white in a classroom in Barcelona. You were wearing dungaree cut-offs and a white t-shirt bearing the words, "Almost Heaven." You were smiling. Your wandering, lazy eye pointed towards your nose. That thatch of red hair thundered from your God-spot like a roaring fire. You were smiling and even though I am now on my blistered knees, I can see who you were before the November ice, before the police tape, the police dogs, and the blue-bloated body I identified in the morgue.

Once, in 1974, you wore a t-shirt ablaze with the words, "Almost Heaven."

That was forty-eight years ago. You were alive then, and we were as hopeful as hummingbirds dancing in the summer sun. We didn't know then how November would break you, or that I would be genuflecting on your bathroom floor, my knees round circles of red as I wiped up your blood, my flesh communing with your ruddy, coagulated spirit, or that I would be whispering, "Almost heaven, brother, almost heaven. Hold on, bro, you're almost there."

There is Nothing New about Grief
Jan Zlotnik Schmidt

There is nothing new about grief.
The way it burns fingers until
they blister or sears through
the body like an electric shock.
The way it leaves traces marks
like white fingerprints on sunburnt
skin or the crust at the corner
of the eye after weeping.

There is nothing new about grief.
The way silence roots in the gullet.
The way you want to yowl
But there are no screams
from a wounded tongue.
At night as cool wind seeps in from
an open window   you are sure you hear
a woman's screech   then you realize it's
coyotes' cacophonous cries and yelps
echoing against dark mountains.

You want sleep   you want oblivion.
No more visions of black rubber body
bags stacked in cooler trucks or faces
masked in blue cloth   eyes staring out
from dimmed television screens.

And then the scratching
almost soundless   creatures
under the sink   in crevices
In the walls   scurrying across
wood planked floors.
You find a carcass of a small
grey mouse in the bathtub
toothpick legs stretched up eyes bloodied.
Into the trash it goes. You ditch it

without a thought. Without mourning.
Without grief. Or so you think.

At night: a graven image of disaster.
And your bloodied hands.

CHAPTER 7

Relationships

Dream: An Angler at One Hundred
Jan Zlotnik Schmidt

If my father were a fisherman, he would dig his crooked toes into the
sand at the shore to make them disappear, a thick tangle of green and
brown seaweed twisting around his ankles. And shards of purple mussels
and waves of indigo and brown clamshells would scrape against his shins,
as the tides rolled in. Then after gazing at the thin white line of the
horizon, he would chisel the fishing pole into a mound of sand, flick the
line with a twitch of his wrist, angle it beyond the waves, a thin curve
of black wire gone into the sea. He'd hold it steady in a high arc, and
occasionally wriggle it a bit to test the waters, to see if fish would snap at
the bait.

But this is all a dream. My Brooklyn father never ventured to the
sea in this way, never watched the glint of sunlight on the waves, never
was satisfied with the infinitesimal arc of the line stretching into the sea.

Instead in the nursing home, I held a conch shell against his ear
and then mine. We listened to the barely audible ebb and flow of tides.
The whorl of the shell against the whorl of his ear. Never uttering a
word, he nodded in time with the tides.

And if I imagined him looking at the sea, gazing into its brightness,
he would be thinking about his own being. As fragile as the skeletal
bones of a fish gnawed at by voracious time. Or maybe he'd be thinking
about his soul—an invisible line into the ocean. Absorbed into some
infinite blue or a path of silver light.

Magical Thinking
Mary K O'Melveny

My Mother was looking for love
long before it ever materialized.
My Father was a failure at it.
For her. Though she never left him.

Years later, I asked why she stayed on,
surrounded by seething anger, as her meager
hopes dwindled to dust. *Options*, she claimed.
For Better Or Worse. But I suspected

she simply hoped love might triumph
after all. When my father was dead,
she re-focused her search, took up
challenges of computerized pairings.

She banged out data on questionnaires
as if she was playing Shostakovich.
Met strangers for coffee. Hiked local trails.
Sipped bourbon and ginger in hotel bars.

Her so-called match lived in Florida.
Off she went, our possessions divided up,
sold in the yard. Later, I learned he was
no better for her than my angry father.

He wore his ugliness like a crown, spit out
venomous commands and watched her gather
them like jewels. They divorced. Reconciled. Parted
again. Lawyers' letters flew like wind-blown leaves.

Eventually, she was free to reach out once more
for romance. This time, ink was her medium.
One Spring day, a finely penned reply, cursive
training evident, arrived on white linen paper.

Alfred lived in Oregon. Loved opera. Laughed
out loud at life's many oddities. Read *The New Yorker*.
Liked her style. A curious visit led to much more.
He moved East. Moved in. *(Neighbors be damned.)*

I still have their picture on my bookshelf.
They are holding hands, leaning to each other,
both laughing. The dog is leaping in the yard.
Even now, their spark sizzles through the frame.

I slowly came to believe in magical thinking
thanks to them. Not simply that happiness
might turn up before all the lights go out
if we wish hard enough. But that it creates

its own power. Alfred died too soon in their story.
Afterwards, each day for a year, my mother wrote
him a letter, speaking as if he were sitting next to her.
Her heart was broken. Love letters kept her alive.

The Song of Doors
Colleen Geraghty

I lay in the bed watching the window, listening to the buzz of summer heat. The soft glow of night reached through the curtain and breathed in and out of the house. I leaned into the street noise: the honk of a horn, the bang of a screen door, the pull-squeak of Mrs. Rafferty's clothesline. She always hung her wash at night.

"It's a sin to go hanging a man's boxers under God's gaze. Let alone letting every sinner see your privates dangling in the wind. God's got enough to do without worrying about my undies flapping in the breeze," she'd say.

Squeak, squeak, Mrs. Rafferty hanging her night wash. Him out on the stoop, smoking and grunting at her as she hoisted her wet sheets, wet undies, every private thing up to the line. Squeak, squeak. Another door slamming. The screech of a car taking the corner too fast. Night buzzed around the window screen, all of us stiff and laid out quiet as corpses in our beds. It had been one hell of a day, him hot
and bothered, his nerves scorched and dangling like bitter fruit off the edge of his tongue, his sour mouth spitting into the morning, slamming into the afternoon, punching a hole through the kitchen wall at supper.

I don't know what had set him off this time, why he woke up whistling. But, before we shoveled the last spoonful of oatmeal into our gullets, he was storming and stomping, and wrecking things. I was too tired to reach back into the day, too tired to empty the broken pieces into the night, too tired to understand God's wild puzzle, or why Nana said, "You gotta be shouldering the burdens girl, keeping your gaze on God."

Squeak, squeak, the line pulled tight on all Mrs. Rafferty's private, unseen and hidden things – all of it pushed closer to the house. His cigarette smoke rose in the heat, bled through the window, lingered over our beds, choked the air so we could barely smell summer. None of us talked, nobody sighed, barely a wiggle out of us, nothing but the night stink of him and us breathless in our beds.

Squeak, squeak, the line pulled tight and, finally, Mrs. Rafferty's "Night." Slam. Her screen door closed behind her and he coughed, me thinking about all the little hidden places I had tucked inside of me.

In the bed, rigid as a corpse, while night lowered herself like a coffin into the dark Philly sky, I listened to the steady tap-tap of Mrs. Rafferty's screen door beating rhythm into night's lonely breeze. The song of that door lulled me into the wonder and the mystery of doors: small doors and big doors, wooden doors, cement doors. Barn doors and shed doors, screen doors and pocket doors, back doors and front doors, kitchen doors and cabinet doors. Dingy, old cellar doors, and stiff oily church doors, the stuffy slick feeling of confessional doors sliding open and closed.

This morning, when he kicked me through the kitchen door and I fell into the grass, he screamed and spit one big pile of shit-flying mess all over me, called me a no-good worthless piece of shit. I didn't know what came next or what flew through the air on the end of his fist, what he said, what he did. I was so busy slamming doors that I lost track of him, lost track of everything but the slam, slam, bang, bang, squeak, squeak of me and Mrs. Rafferty hiding everything we didn't want nobody else to see.

I knew doors like my blood knew my veins, knew my bones, my skin. I knew the hidden things locked behind my eyes. I knew how some doors bolted from the inside. I knew the song of doors.

A Tryst Near Hobart, New York

Tana Miller

shortly after leaving Hobart   a hamlet reminiscent
of villages conjured by a child from miniature
Sugar Pops cereal boxes   I spotted
a muddy hoof-print-riddled field teeming
with Holstein cows   some entirely red
others white or delicately piebald   many displaying
an imaginary continent imprinted on a blank flank   I pulled
to the roadside   excited   eagerly crossed the road for a chat
the ladies swished long fringe at the end of their tails
as some stood with small groups of special friends   others
wove around the cliques or traversed the field from end-to-end
many snorted the morning air   nostrils flared
some pawed the slick ground
nuzzled others   touched noses   all appeared genial

one rangy individual   an inland sea embossed on her side
sashayed over to greet me   her sharp-boned rectangular body
gangly   her bag a wrinkled leather balloon   I reached forward
caressed the top of her bumpy head   she pushed her face closer
so I could stroke her hairless pink & grey nose
our eyes locked
we stood together for a long long time

at last I whispered   *I have to go*
thanks for coming   she said   *I get lonesome sometimes*
me too   I murmured
drive ever so carefully my love   she said

MORE AND MOST BETT (OR)

Eileen Howard

More and most bett(or)
than a heroin habit
YOU
(are the Magic Rabbit)
that jumps
out of my head at importunate
and sometimes
unfortunate
times
& beguiles
my body &
mind with
soft whodunit
mysteries
of impudent
desire and
raillery.

Frail barque,
this is not the
time
for such thoughts
and longings:
Cloister yourselves!!

Prurient petal mongers
they--
floating on
a sea of amused
indifference--
& I
twist and
turn
on their
crazy breezes
and listen

to their
amused
shy sneezes.
It does me
nothing to
carp at these
Rorschach
foreigners—
as the blood runs
wily
into unprotected
corners—
as thoughts fly
fleetingly
playing forbidden
horns or
traipsing—
most intransigent
& guileless.

It's an amusement
most feckless
wild
and
wily, and
dyed in all the
crazy pigments
of terpsichore (to name a dance).
—I don't know
the rune,
but morning or
noon
this
(uncalled for)
imp of desire
and
remembered pleasures
steeped in
All Your Specifics

can step
coyly
down
my back bone
right out
to other
focal
centers
& sit there—(laughing.)

I Heart You, Honey
Kappa Waugh

I'm searching the ultra-romantic section,
puffy satin hearts, starched lace: "Dot
your signature scent here," the insert
suggests. Hmm, do they mean my cologne
or pheromones from my private parts?
Maybe not the tone I want to strike. He is
a gas-station-flowers kind of guy. He invariably
picks alstroemeria, cheaper than roses
and a flower I can't abide.

Let's move on to the humorous. Here's one, a
colorful lizard, captioned "Iguana hold your
hand." Well, I'm a Beatles fan, but he really
likes the Clancy Brothers more. Wonder if
they have one saying, "I love you more than
'Danny Boy' or Irish whiskey?"

How about a kid's card? I grab one showing
kittens in a basket. The caption: "You're PURRfect,
Valentine." But 1) he isn't, and 2) he hates
cats, and 3) he threw up on my (ironic)
"Hello, Kitty" sofa pillow, so I had to toss it.

Back at the humor section, I see a misplaced
Romantic. Flowery script: "Dear Valentine. . ."
I open it and think, "YES!"
Inside is simply: "Go to Hell!"

Bosom Buddies
Jan Zlotnik Schmidt

> *We'll always be bosom buddies*
> *Friends, neighbors, and pals.*
> Mame

As my husband plays "Bosom Buddies" from *Mame* on YouTube on
his IPAD, as Angela Lansbury and Bea Arthur do a soft shoe across
the Tony stage, my mind flashes back to visions of my mother and her
best friend, Mildred: scenes of the two women arguing on the phone,
hugging at Chanukah, dousing each other with vituperative remarks,
and then making up. Seventy years of the ups and downs of a friendship
that started when my mother sat behind Mildred in a French class at
Brooklyn College--the "W" girls--my mother's maiden name Weintraub,
Mildred's, Wolfe. Two women who remained friends and enemies until
my mother's death in 2009. Like the two warring and loving buddies
in *Mame*, my mother and Mildred were glib, forceful, biting when they
wanted to be, and loving when they needed to be.

Mildred would brag about her fancy fur maker who made her mink
coat, and my mother would retort that her lambswool jacket was just as
nice, as she privately told her family: "She always has to have the best,
even with peaches or apples." "She has to go to Blue Ribbon, the fancy
fruit market or The Lox Box for bagels and smoked salmon." And after
my mother's death, I finally had to agree with her when we took Mildred
to buy grapes at the market, and she fingered and grazed each green
grape, looking for the perfect bunch without any brown tinge.

Theirs was a friendship based on competition and unswerving
dedication to each other. My mother would complain that Mildred
always had to have the fanciest clothes and shoes. Her husband, Jerry,
would take her to the Lower East Side where she'd buy designer suits
at Forman's, and my mother would go bargain shopping at May's or
Loehmann's. My mother was jealous that Jerry, a lawyer, could shower
Mildred with gifts of diamond rings and ruby necklaces—jewelry my
father couldn't afford to get her.

It was obvious why my mother was envious of Mildred, but I never knew why Mildred had to "one up" my mother. I thought maybe it went back to their Brooklyn College days, so I searched for clues in the *Broeklundian*, their 1935 senior yearbook. I found out |that my mother, a natural leader, was chancellor of her sorority, President of the History Club, a varsity hockey player, and a member of various college committees while Mildred only had a sorority and Le Cercle Francais next to her name. Did Mildred feel then as if she couldn't measure up to my mother, couldn't match my mother's successes? Was this the source of her initial jealousy and rivalry with her? I, of course, will never know for sure.

I do know that they both bore responsibility for the tumult in their relationship. They accused each other of being stubborn and needing to win every argument. Mildred would complain that my mother always had to be right. One time they argued about balloons:

"Mildred, you love balloons. Every luncheon has thousands of balloons." You said, "You have to love a balloon."

"Mae, I never would say that. I would never say 'I loved a balloon.'"

This bickering marked the many phases of their friendship. In my mother's last years, when her dementia escalated, they'd argue about every date they got together, every trip they took as couples. "It was the Panama Canal, when you fell, Mill," OR "It was in China that you got so sick." And Mildred would counter, "No, NO, it was on our trip to the Bahamas." The arguments could go on for days, in person, and on the phone. In my mother's last months, Mildred, irritated, confided in me: "Your mother is so stubborn. She's always wrong you know." Her sons and I would say, "Please don't argue. It's Mae's dementia." But Mildred could not stop herself from a pattern of behavior, programmed into her over the course of seventy years.

They also knew exactly what to say to hurt each other; they knew each other's tender spot and how to rub it raw. Mildred, always envious that my mother had daughters, while she had two sometimes solicitous sons who were close to their father—the three men all loved classical music and played violin and piano in an orchestra--mourned that loss. Not close to her daughters-in-law, she always stoked my mother's pride in her children by saying, "You're lucky. Your girls take care of you." But then her viperous tongue came out. Once during the free love era of the late 60s, when I was in college, I met Mildred in a doctor's office where she was seeing her psychiatrist, and I was going to the gynecologist to get birth control pills. At a family dinner soon after, at the Homestead, as we were chomping on rib eyes, she turned to me and said, "Getting a little chubby. Your upper arms look thick. You are fleshy around the middle. Hmmmmm any change in your diet?" At the time I didn't want to tell my mother I was sexually active since I had no steady boyfriend. Boyfriend the term used then. Later my mother, figuring out my secret, confronted me: "What were you doing there? Why buy the cow if you can get the milk for free?" Mildred got me in trouble and caused my mother undue anguish.

My mother also could be a bit vicious. When Mildred's son, Steve, lost his job at the hospital where he was an internist, my mother often questioned her at bridge parties, in front of their mutual friends, "So how is Steve doing? It must be so hard for him. Losing his job at his time in life." And Mildred would cringe because she was both worried about his job prospects and ashamed her Jewish doctor son whom she often bragged about had lost his position.

The longest period that my mother and Mildred were angry at each other involved Hillary Clinton. As President of the Brooklyn Chapter of the National Council of Jewish Women (quite a progressive organization as opposed to the more traditional Hadassah), Mildred invited Hillary to speak at East Midwood Jewish Center when the latter was running for Senator while Bill was President. Mildred presided over the event: doing publicity and orchestrating the session. As she stood in the back of the meeting room, she watched my mother sidle up to Hillary, lean into her, and give her advice as my mother later reported: "Hillary you should run for President." The next day my cousins in Washington, D.C. called me, chuckling: "Guess who is on the front page of *The Washington Post*: Your mother." There she was in her blue silk blouse in a seemingly intimate conversation with the First Lady. "Senior citizen greets Hillary" was the caption. Mildred was furious. My mother, gloating over her triumphant moment, made multiple copies of the photo, framed them, and gave them to all her friends including Mildred. They had the capacity to twist the knife in, to cause small wounds that wouldn't heal.

Theirs were seventy years of cycles of competing and causing trouble, then being loyal and supportive. There were New Year's gatherings, bridge evenings, Chanukah parties with delicious latkes, Bar and Bat Mitzvahs, weddings, and naming ceremonies. The daily life of shared meals, shared gossip, and shared help. After Jerry died, Mildred called my mother in the middle of the night, complaining that she couldn't sleep. My mother and father went over to her apartment in Brooklyn, not far from their home, and sat with her until the morning. But then, before they left, she argued with Mildred, "Why didn't you take Tylenol PM? What's wrong with you?" This was not the way to comfort someone who's grieving I later told her when she reported what she had said.

Why were women of that generation so competitive with each other, and at the same time, so devoted and loving? I've often thought that in an era in which psychotherapy was a sign of weakness, these two strong women who couldn't engage in introspection, redirected their feelings of disappointment and loss into jealousy and competition. I know my mother often felt that my father wasn't successful enough, that they weren't wealthy enough, although my parents led a comfortable, financially secure existence throughout their lives, even though they struggled in the 1950s when I was little and teachers' salaries were low. Mildred certainly had a wonderful marriage and a giving and loving husband as well as financial security. So what caused the sniping? Perhaps both of them, strong women, felt less independent, more dependent on their husbands, and, in some way silenced, although they led productive lives as professional women. My mother was an Assistant Principal and Chair of a Social Studies Department of thirty men and two women; Mildred was a Math teacher and then Math Specialist, training other elementary school teachers. They were not "stay at home" moms. Perhaps the silencing came from their immigrant backgrounds or their sense that their husbands "ruled the roost." Or perhaps this was just their atavistic way of asserting themselves and exercising power. I will never know. Despite their acid tongues, their friendship endured for over seventy years.

I remember that last time Mildred saw my mother. Her son, Eliot, drove her from her retirement home in Westchester, the assisted living complex she despised, to our family home where my mother was in hospice just a month before she died. The two women sat together, holding hands--their pink manicured fingers entwined. They sat quietly, smiling at each other, their bodies close, shoulder to shoulder. Girls again. Women again. Old women together for the last time. They talked of all their times together, like pages in a movie flip book. An evening of bridge. A dinner at Mario's in Brooklyn. Their times at Palisades State Park when they were young, took the ferry, and hiked the trails-- the four of them not yet married (I couldn't imagine any of them hiking), the days at the bungalow colony playing mah-jong, the cruises. Shoulder to shoulder. Then they stopped talking. They sat in silence for a while, Mildred stroking my mother's forearm. My mother looked at her with an unflinching gaze as if she knew that this was the end. Finally, Mildred had to leave and with tears in her eyes turned to me, "I know this will be the last time."

My mother died a month later. Mildred lived another two years. My husband and I often visited her in the retirement home and took her out for cheeseburgers or cheesecake--foods that she thought were awful at the complex. She would always say, "You were a good girl. You were a good daughter." The woman who had a venomous streak had softened and gave me the nurturing and affirmation I longed for.
Now they are both gone. I feel unmoored, as if some essential foundation of my life has crumbled. What is left is the sense that I am on unsteady ground, not knowing where my next step will take me or where I will fall.

In the middle of the night when I can't sleep, I think how lucky these two women were to have a friendship that lasted a lifetime. They knew despite their trivial arguments that they still were those girls, the two W's sitting in that French class, determined to be "bosom buddies and pals."

Stork Stories
Mary K O'Melveny

...For Oona and Esme

My godchild has given birth to a baby
girl, her second child. The birth was
smooth and relatively swift. Kate's
own birth took much longer than a day.
We were all so young when we gathered
to celebrate beside the stone fireplace in my
Woodstock living room. We bore poems,
feathers, crystals and champagne. We were
filled with moral certainties, predictions for
our lives based on little more than nerve.

I find it is impossible not to think of storks.
those legendary bearers of good tidings, luck,
who transport the newly hatched in their wide
beaks. Old legends say that babies will come
if sweet treats are left to rest on windowsills.
In Spain, nesting pairs of white storks fill up
rooftops. They sweep and glide through the sky
like seasoned flamenco dancers, their calls
to mate reverberating like castanets.

Each year, these storks migrate from Spain
to Africa and back. In one day, they can
travel four hundred kilometers. They leave
behind sun-drenched savannahs, sweep past
the Black Sea, the Bosporus Straits, sail
on warm winds until they reach a roost they
knew before. This is my wish for both great
goddaughters – to catch each updraft,
to free-wheel as wetlands mirror a sunrise,
to always trust there is a safe landing point.

For My Father on Yom Kippur—Two Years After His Passing

Jan Zlotnik Schmidt

(Wellfleet, Massachusetts)

I wish I could have seen your life like the ebb and flow of tides.
The water's edge damp with pocked green and brown seaweed gathering
in pools at the shore.
Seen the hermit crab crawl out of its shell, skitter across the beach, seen
its bubbles of breath,
and the shards of purple mussels and white clam shells.
Signs of past life dredged up from the sea.   Fissures in a death march.
I wish I could have seen your ebbing soul, your gripped lips, your lidded
closed eyes, and imagined a life beyond your shrouded
shriveled self.
Pared down to thin bones and wrinkled sleep not spirit.
That would have been a beginning back to you.
Back to your ebbing soul, your closed eyes, a life beyond dust,
back to love.
I wish I had heard the unheard like murmurs of unseen waves.
Heard whispers in your gasps of being.
I wish I had noticed a crack in space, in time, remembering not your
unknowing, my unknowing, but the presence of the unsaid
on your lips.
Now I wish I could dream you whole, dream you alive.
Dream you with me.
And imagine our breath mingling among the stars.

Two Leaves

Kappa Waugh

Two leaves play a waiting game.
They tremble, imitating weakness
in the light wind, the cold sunlight;
which one will give up first?

Something I have not done since
fifty years ago, with our young child,
look and listen for signs of life, the
rise & fall of chest, stir of limbs.

Now, slipping back in bed, after the
bladder call of dawn, I study your
beloved body to see if you survived
the night. Reassured, I curl to sleep.

CHAPTER 8

Aging and Health

Gray Is More Than An Absence of Color: A Haibun
Mary K O'Melveny

My hair turned silver twenty-five years ago. The first strands of
pearled gray likely settled down like ash as I stared at my office
telephone one afternoon as if it had been dropped by aliens into my
hand. It's *malignant* said the disembodied male voice on the line (in the
same timbre that had assured me through test after test that there was no
cause for worry). His words swept over me like wind-blown
first frost leaves. I walked down the hallway to see if the third eye of
fright painted on my forehead was visible to others, but it was not. Over
the course of weeks, months, each lock of my hair slowly shed
any pretense of color, turned pale as a slant of light on early snow. Over
the years, some asked (often in slightly hushed tones) if I had considered
"coloring" my hair – *to make you look younger. No,* I
always declared -- *I earned every one of these!* Each fine, moonshine-filled
filament represented a rogue cell banished by its pale turn. My gray hairs
evidenced discarded fears. The way water birds suddenly
rise up from the sea in a cloud before disappearing into a dusky sky.
A brief upheaval before stillness returns, leaving my thoughts steeled
toward survival instead of loss.

> **Shadows can haunt us**
> **or gift us with lambent light**
> **to cloak our worst fears**

Retirement

Kappa Waugh

Our old-age home houses
has-been hermit bandits.
We sidle from our cells,
masked, we edge down
blue-flowered corridors
to grab our mail, refills
of pills, then head back
to our hideouts on Floor 3,
740 square feet, a bland
and pleasant den. Our old
nemeses are gone, defanged,
disarmed. The Lone Ranger
is in the Memory Unit, Tonto
moved home to Oklahoma,
and Dale died last year.
Daily the secret knock; grub's
here. Tuesday's turkey with
sage stuffing brings back a
whiff of days of desperado
derring-do. Where are the
neighs of yesteryear? Trigger
turned to cat food long ago,
yet I hear the ghostly clip-
clop as the horseman rides
the corridor of blue flowers.

When We Lay in the Grass
Tana Miller

while the sky glowed peach
along its far edges & shadows morphed
trees into whiskery shapes   I propped
my head on one hand   stretched out
in front of your chicken coop   the hens
slept in their nests   your two cats
stalked mice   insects   we nestled
in the damp grass like wild things
much softer   more innocent
still   we were grown women who should
have recognized the danger we faced
we were young then   much younger

now   we are too busy   distracted
to linger in unmown grass
the chicken coop is gone
a vicious attack killed the hens
Trixie & Virgil   the two cats you brought
from the city thirty years ago
are buried near that spot with my son's rabbit
we are both still here   but we are different
as is the grass   tended now

Thoughts of a Dying Woman
Kit Goldpaugh

it's a cargo train
or the night wind howling over the Hudson
      it might be a dog

she and her father visited a goat farm
once   the lady in white is a nurse
  a goat hopped up and ate the roses on her dress

a bird in the window twitches, pecks and sits
the feeder is empty
     behind the bird
          in the abandoned branches of an oak   another black
                                        bird descends

there was a woman   in her attic   once   more than once
she glowed white in the window frame
        or was the light hers   her gossamer hair
           that iridescent blue silk sarong
               draped over the black oak chest
                 on which she sat
     this attic   one minute filled with small cases pearls and gold
        in velvet lined mahogany   then gone
          like the wind in her window now

it's snowing   something is moving under the pear tree

     it's snowing now   outside   halos in headlights
          on streetlights   on porches
            undisturbed by the gathering spirits of snow

Going Our Way

Kappa Waugh

My family moved toward Death in different ways.
One grandfather I never met, so forgot himself before dying,
he never even knew he was walking in Death's direction. His
wife fought her escort every inch of the way, tried to bring her
silver wine goblets along. No luck. My other grandmother,
the good one, the one who loved Jesus with such Kentucky girl
flirtatiousness, you'd think His name was written on her
dance card. She was so wild to reach Him, they tied her hands
to the hospital bed, so she couldn't pull out her IV. Her husband
died quiet and sober as a judge. Judge was his nickname, poet
and corporation lawyer. He loved & judged us too. We were
found wanting, but Death wanted him, as it wants us all.
My mother, poet's daughter, poet herself, wrote Death sonnets,
imagined for herself an end like Anna K.'s, down by the train
tracks, but in the end, she couldn't trek that far. My dad was in a
rush; he used a bullet to speed him on his way. And I ask
myself how will I approach that door? Skipping with
curiosity? Will that kill the Kat?

The Glint in Parchment

Jan Zlotnik Schmidt

It was the money plant that pointed the way. The brown stems were brittle and ready to snap at the touch, and the pods thinned like a layer of flaking, tanned skin. But I grabbed a branch, broke the stalk, shook it, the brown flat seeds floating into my open palm. I peeled the sheath of another small parchment oval away and there was a slight glimmer, a hint of muted pearl like a single streak of white light on a gray sea.

It was the money plant that pointed the way. I remember searching for it in bramble and weeds, in blackberry patches, and stands of glossy evergreen bushes. It pushed its way out into the air, ready to be plucked. My son at three tugged the brown stalks until they gave way, and then he held the cool silk oval to his cheek, soft as tissue paper. And I remember that we both carefully pulled away the outer browned layers and there was the silver, untouched, glimmering in the sun. That was thirty years ago.

And later each time when I went to the bay, when my son was five and seven and thirteen, we searched for the money plant, looked for it against gray picket fences, weeds on the side of the road, stands of rose hips. We looked for it as the ocean turned violet, midnight, or fresco blue, but the plant was not there. It had disappeared. The floating seeds and silver white discs gone.

Then I return to a cottage by the sea when I am sixty-five, return to watch the light on the bay. The flecks of silver turned to liquid streaks that sparked in the sun. A vision that brought delight and awe. A comfort at a time when the only certainty was flux and change. I accept so much even the ache in my gut. The friends lost to cancer, the mother gone, the lost son gone from home, a wanderer never to return. I see them. Their shadows passing through my body in nightmares. The screams of my mother, her leaden shuffle before death; the blank eyes of my father in the midst of dementia; the friend's crow-like voice on the telephone days before he died. These memories flood my mind as I stare at the sea.

I walk back to the cottage, expecting nothing. Then I see it. The money plant, darkened by fall, more brittle than in early summer. I break off a stem, peel the browned film away---peel each side carefully because there are cuts in the oval, and some pods are broken and ragged. I find one untouched by wind or rain. Pull away the sheaths. And there it is. A small parchment oval. Yellow white with a hint of silver. I break off several more that are intact. And when I blow against the pods, they rustle but don't crack off the stems. They flutter in the air like translucent wings.

The money plant points the way.
A silver sheen that stops my breath.
A glint that erases time.

Some Things You Should Know About Me
Tana Miller

some things you should know about me:
I have lived   well-and-not-so-well
in the same house for almost forty years
it's not a house I chose
not a convenient house
not a luxurious house
not historical
the house hosts in season:
      ants   tiny to huge
      ladybugs   especially in the upstairs bathroom
      stink bugs   some decades more plentiful than others
      mice   at times in huge abundance
      rats (once) years ago
      a scruffy cat with crusty eyes we named Miky
      & later found out was named Butch & lived down the street
another thing you should know: my house sits
on a half-circle street crowded
nose-to-nose with other non-notable houses
twenty years ago   the final argument
between the couple across the street blared
through the neighborhood like a hurricane warning
another thing I should admit:
when I was clipping the Rose-of-Sharon bushes
I heard sounds of love making
from my neighbor's screened porch
I froze   stood perfectly still like a doe in a field
nose twitching   until they finished
she's young   a single mother   I was pleased for her
the most important thing you should know:
I have come to deeply love
the carnival-following   dollar-store-frequenting
shirt-factory-laboring   country-music-blasting family next door
who compliment my potato salad   guard our house when we're away

dig holes for new bushes   re-installed the mailbox three times
shovel snow from our walk   pry painted-closed windows open
love our dog as much as we do   keep an eye out for our grumpy cat
bring food when we are sick
I sit on my rocker on the front porch
of my crooked little house on my tight little street
and grow contentedly old   older

CHAPTER 9

Bearing Witness in a Darkened World

The Dalai Lama Says
Eileen Howard

turn off the news

b r e a t h e

let everything   quiet become

let synapses mellow

let yourself   float   in a

pool   of reflection

body   dissolves   disappears

hum of the universe   soothes

dragonflies' loop-de-loops

tadpoles' somersaults

morning mist

ethereal call of a mourning dove

leaves rustling in the wind

Escape

for awhile

b r e a t h e

Fragile
Kit Goldpaugh

in March
hours before we pulled up the drawbridge and shut down
my doctor gave me a box of nearly new women's shoes
       size 7 ½
for the shelter   or the shop   or. . . from his wife
who died quite suddenly   I knew her from high school
when he slid the box of shoes into my car
      he said   she hated shoes
      I remember her Birkenstocks
          we embraced   a tiny buffer between anguish
and the next breath

the neatly packed shoes wait in my closet for now
      the seeds I planted in eggshells in March are tomato plants
         I feel fragile   sometimes
      like the spider-crack on my computer screen
      like a fault line
      like a land mine

Testing The Limits of Art
Mary K O'Melveny

"Can Art Save Us?" my friend asks.
He argues, of course, that it can.
It must. It will.
There is reason and there is spirit.
Ideas can be brought to joyous, thriving life.
People talking, thinking, reaching out
across impossible borders, sparks
flying brightly across dark boundaries,
sounds of clapping hands
turning into holding hands,
morphing into songs or poems
about peace and love.

I wanted to believe in this
when we walked past the Belfast walls,
filled with hopeful messages
scrawled below the stark razor wire.
Sidewalk curbs painted bright with colors
so you will know which side you are on
when the walled gates slam shut at six p.m.
Gaza has them too.
Though they do not ever open easily
at least for one side.
There are people in these places who see music
as a ladder, optimism climbing up and over,
a trajectory of communities in positive motion.
The Belfast murals, the shuttered desert enclosures,
the not so invisible dividing lines in the dirt
may call out a different tune altogether.

Oh I do so want to believe in the power
of pens and batons and brushes
to save everyone. But I worry
that the redemptive energy of music and art
is a First World dream.

A woman suddenly drops
onto a South Sudan street
from a hunger so great
she has left her children far behind her.
At the hospital where she is taken,
she is not even an unusual case.
In fact, she will be quickly released. And die.
There will be no funeral march.
No drumming or soft *a capella* mourning songs.

I want to embrace the salvational capacity
of imaginative beings.
If only we could sing food into existence,
use bursts of raw color to replace gunshots,
write poems that warring leaders would recite
to each other in the honesty of the stark night.
What if the woman on the street
had a story in her head
that was not about starvation at all?
What if she had been mixing melodies and harmonies
into a joyous idea of survival?
And she was standing here to tell us all
how to rejoice in still being alive?
This would be the purest magic.
Or perhaps the simple purity
of creative magical thinking.
Oh yes   I want to believe.

Weapons of Mass Instruction
Kappa Waugh

At 6:30 that evening, Jamie Denton, of Marfa, Texas, had a twelve-point buck in his sights. He pulled the trigger, and...nothing. No bang, no kick of the stock against his shoulder, nothing. Yes, safety off, yes, Browning 700 loaded. It was as if the gun had died.

Tim Kincaid, an Upland, California car salesman, took the last step in his increasing violence against his wife, Nancy. His 40-caliber pistol, although pointed at Nancy, misfired, destroying eight of the twenty-seven bones of his right hand.

A stash of hoarded RUAG-made hand grenades in a Syrian backwater turned very quietly to dust and small metal fragments, causing an Isis cell to scatter to the four quarters of the Gulf.

That same day, the little green lights on the president's 'football,' ready to speed nuclear warheads on their way, flickered and went out. The revolt of the weapons had begun.

At first, firearms remained responsive to women's touch. Armed forces in countries that fielded female soldiers scaled down enormously, but most of the troops were dissatisfied with the unhappy mess of war, and many claimed their weapons weren't working right, rifles jerking when fired, and who started this stupid war anyway, with fellow women and children suffering more than the enemy soldiers, also mostly women by this time. A few men attempted workarounds, dressing as women, and carrying lucky women's trigger fingers on a keychain. But the guns knew. Girl gangs in the big cities enjoyed a brief cachet, but male gang members weren't happy giving the girls that power, and the gangs turned their main energies to tagging and doing the dozens. All over the world, guns changed their makeup, turning to taffy, to powder, to brittle. Where large amounts of guns were gathered together, like armories, the collections took on a fecal quality, both in feel and odor. Wars eventually drifted into uniform contests and battles of the bands, with the United Nations as judges of the competition.

Since escalation of violence had been the general direction of mankind since Hammurabi, this de-escalation threw a switch in the human brain. Peace talks actually resulted in increased peace. Game shows featuring humor competitions flourished, while books and movies about war took on the tone of mild pornography. And while children still played king or queen of the mountain, none of them *pointed their fingers to say, "Bang, Bang, you're dead!"*

Excavating My Mind
Eileen Howard

Why am I pulled, strangling,
from my dreams into an
inky night filled with horrors...
The news blares from a
silenced TV, rips into my psyche
promising death, destruction,
and global meltdown.
Handmaids in black bonnets
blow buildings into smoking
rubble, fighter jets honoring
our valiant health care workers
go rogue: attack each other,
plummet from the sky into
innocent crowds below.
In my mind, chaos rules
and an angry cartoon Trump
hops up and down,
trampling through my dreams.

On Zoom, my mouth
is stuffed with cotton.
What matters some ancient prophet's
trials? Who can
concentrate as
the concrete sets,
cementing us into our separate,
distant-flung islands?

Center of the World: (About Larry Blair's Photograph of a House in New Mexico)

Jan Zlotnik Schmidt

This is the center of the world
she says.
But she doesn't notice
the scorched desert sands
the cracks in the adobe walls
the tears in the thin parched skin of the world.

This is the center of the world
she says.
And she doesn't notice the way
the horizontal white lines of the roof
never meet or the way two
stripes form a hex a portent of disaster.

She doesn't remember red clay or dust
or her fingers digging and scratching
in soil for signs of water. If this is
the way it was she says it is all
forgotten. The dryness on her tongue.
The arid stretches of land.

The memory of arroyos and creeks
that once widened into a blue
haze of waters. Rain flooding her heart.

Now this must be the
earth's center.
The fragrant spill of pine or locust
the pale peach squares
of light the strips of wood framing
earth and sky.

She bows to the single bare tree
in the courtyard. Trunk thin as white birch
reaching to the edge of a world.

What Women Carry*
Colleen Geraghty

What had she carried in the swell of her belly from a breakfast of coffee and toast, bright egg yolk nesting now like a small sunburst on the edge of her lip?

What had she carried in the deep well of her heart when he plugged six bullets into the back of her skull? What rose up in her throat as she hit the floor, mouth open as he stomped the red rose of her head into a crumpled pile of bones and blood?

What pulsed inside the folds of her tongue when her teeth embedded in the hard wood of the floor, left standing like tiny tombstones after the police finally arrived, rolled her soft body over to see if she was still a wife, a mother of two, or a corpse?

Her daughter stepped her small feet, one shoe on, one shoe off, over her mother's bloody body when he hollered for her to get him a glass of water.

Her baby brother carried his six-year-old-tears to the phone, pushing 911 like his now silent mother had told him to do, "if, if, if, there was ever a time when you might need it."

The little girl carried the trembling glass, sloshing water into the red river pooling around her mother's silent limbs, handing it to him.

He quenched his thirst.

She bent down, touched her small hand to the floor, innocent fingers mingling with water and the red river pooling around her mother's thick crown of hair.

"There is nothing," St. Teresa's whispers carried through prayer, "which puts the devils to flight like holy water."

"Mama, my Mama," her baby brother's sobs lift into the rafters of the house like a million shrieking birds.

The man, their mother's husband, their father, still grips his gun in his right hand. His screams shoot over his son's shoulder penetrating through the airwaves to the dispatcher: "I just shot my wife six times in the back of the head. I just shot my wife six times in the back of the head."

"Mama, my Mama, she's bleeding. Come quick!"

I carried the vision of four front teeth, embedded in the hardwood floor, as they turned this mother face up and pronounced her dead in front of her wailing children.

I still carry a purple ribbon of remembrance for all the women dead and gone, killed by an intimate partner. I carried a purple ribbon on my shirt collar, my heavy heart thudding inside the hollow of my chest, sobs choking in my throat.

I carried my heavy, heavy heart.

I carry it around with me every single day.

*In the United States, three woman die every day at the hands of an intimate partner. 94% of female murder victims are killed by men they know.
(National Domestic Violence Hotline: 1-800-SAFE)

Michelangelo's Breath
Eileen Howard

Winter storms fade away.
Mars' dust rages across
a lonely planet.
It's been ages since I
embraced your so familiar
body. Now I do aught but
keen a desolate threnody.

Space dust, captured by
our beleaguered planet
sifts down necks,
comingles with sweat
containing molecules
of Michelangelo's breath:
limps across Earth,
dives through crocodiles'
noses. One supposes
all will right itself
in time.

It Must Have a Name
Kit Goldpaugh

It must have a name   this awful thing   this thing that visits that falls
　　　　like snow in Chernobyl　　　it stays　　it seeps
　　　　　　　　it sits   it doesn't lift   it sits   it shifts the air
　　　　　　　　　　　or something in it
　　　　　　　　or something in you
　　　　　　　　something cellular
　　　　It's that disturbance
　　　　　　　　growing like an idea   that feeling   the burning
　　　　　　　　light radiating
　　　　　　　　from Thich Quang Duc's body
It must have a name this uninvited　　palpable thing

　　　　　　　　　　　　　　　　that everyone says
　　　　you can feel in the air　　　　in Venice　　in Dublane　　in
　　　　Newtown
　　　　in the very air of Sierra Leone　　　Guyana　　　　Spain
　　　　Sub-Saharan Africa

on the TV　　the graph lines climb gondolas bang in canals
　　　　　　　　　　　　　　　a planet pauses
It's here
　　　　　　　in the empty streets of Ecuador,
　　　　　　　in a meat-packing factory
　　　　　　　on the banks of the Big Sioux River
It must have a name this awful thing　　　that's too late to stop
like the man who notices the sea retreating　　　　　and says
　　　　　　　　　　　　　　　too late

　　　TSUNAMI
or Lot　　　who warns his wife　　too late　　　don't look back.

Mourning Dove Portfolios

Mary K O'Melveny

Outside my window, four doves converse
on spider webs of oak and maple branches.
Fattened by bird seed, they peer out
over the long-wintered meadow
like savvy scouts searching the scenery
for signs of trouble ahead.

I want to call out that trouble, indeed,
has arrived. The work of doves has never
been as necessary. As they shake
out their grey feathers against these
sharp winds, I am betting on savvy
instinct. Times of rest have ended.

Our Capitol is under siege. Crowds
of crazies have climbed granite walls,
swept past barricades, spit on floors,
pushed through hallways as they dove
for crumbs tossed out by a madman.
No one gave much thought to doves.

Some days I can hear their whistle –
a high-pitched whine from their wings
designed to scare off predators. Their
pigeon relatives flew messages for kings
and armadas, Caesar and Genghis Kahn.
Imagine the noise they must have made.

Most doves have ten thousand feathers.
In a dream I watched as flocks circled the mall,
wings whinnying beneath a pale sun.
In the beating, bleating air, fluff, tufts,
plumage sifted down, cushioned the ground.
Soon silence was everywhere. Soft as snow.

Biographies

Colleen Geraghty

Colleen is a certified Amherst Writers and Artist Facilitator and founder of The Hudson Valley Story Cottage, a creative space for writers. Her work has appeared in *Walkill Valley Writers Anthologies 2012/2013* and in *Slant of Light: Contemporary Women Writers of the Hudson Valley, Poems From Wellspring (2019)* as well as in *An Apple In Her Hand (Co-author).* Colleen's poetry has also appeared in *Voice of Eve, Psyche Journal, Chronogram and Lightwood Press.com.* She was the winner of the Hudson Valley Writer's Guild 2013 Short Story Contest. Colleen is also an acclaimed musician and songwriting instructor. Two songs from her CD Deep Ravine ("Hymn for Matthew" and "Nikolay") have been widely used by educators and community groups to raise awareness about hate crimes and PTSD. Colleen was the recipient of Ulster County's 2014 "Raising Hope Award" for mentoring.

Kit Goldpaugh

Kit taught writing for over for over thirty years in the Hudson Valley to students ranging in age from middle school to college. Her work has appeared in *An Apple In Her Hand (Co-author).* Over that time, she participated in the Bard Institute for Thinking and Writing program, the Hudson Valley Writers Workshop and was awarded both a FIPSI summer grant on composition and an NEH fellowship on Women and Fiction. She lives in the People's Republic of Rosendale with her husband, where they raised four sons.

Eileen Howard

Eileen grew up in an Oklahoma university town, one of four siblings, all of whom spent their childhoods camping every summer with their parents. She went to Scripps College in Claremont, California and had a daughter in Hawaii and a son in Halifax, Nova Scotia before landing in New England where she went back to school to become a psychiatric nurse. Eileen worked in both hospital settings and in home care before her retirement. Eileen is an active writer and photographer. Her work has appeared *An Apple In Her Hand (Co-author)*, and on national blog sites such as *Writing in a Woman's Voice* and *Global Poemic* and in literary journals. She has been a featured reader at local Hudson Valley events.

Tana Miller

During a thirty-year teaching career, Tana authored language curriculum guides for her school district, co-founded and facilitated a grade 5-8 annual literary magazine, presented Whole Language workshops in Hudson Valley public schools and at the New York State Reading Conference, for which she received a commendation from the local literacy foundation. Tana co-founded and participated for ten years as a volunteer in a book group at Danbury Federal Prison for Women in Danbury, Connecticut. Tana's work has been published in several feminist and literary journals and in *A Woman's Voice, Slant of Light* (Codhill Press) and *An Apple In Her Hand (Co-author)* (Codhill Press). Tana was a selected reader at the Newark Public Library and has been a featured reader at local gatherings, libraries and book stores.

Mary K O'Melveny

A retired labor rights lawyer living with her wife near Woodstock, New York and in Washington DC, Mary's poetry has appeared in print and on-line journals, including *FLARE: The Flagler Review, The Offbeat, Slippery Elm Literary Journal, Into the Void, West Texas Review, Think, Hamilton Stone Review, Passager Literary Journal, Minerva Rising, Split Rock Review, The Poet's Billow, An Apple In Her Hand (Co-author)* and *The Write Place at the Write Time,* as well as in many anthologies and on various national blog sites such as *The New Verse News* and *Writing in a Woman's Voice.* Her poems have won or been finalists in several national and international poetry competitions and she has been nominated for the Pushcart Press Prize Series. Mary is the author of *A Woman of a Certain Age, Merging Star Hypotheses* (Finishing Line

Press 2018, 2020) and *Dispatches From The Memory Care Museum* (Kelsay Books 2021). She is a co-author of *An Apple in Her Hand* (Cahill Press-2019).

Jan Zlotnik Schmidt

A SUNY Distinguished Teaching Professor Emerita in the Department of English at SUNY New Paltz, Jan's work has been published in many journals including *Kansas Quarterly, The Alaska Quarterly Review, Memoir (and),* and *The Broadkill Review.* Her work has been nominated for the Pushcart Press Prize Series. She has had two volumes of poetry published by the Edwin Mellen Press (*We Speak in Tongues,* 1991; *She had this memory,* 2000). Her chapbook, *The Earth Was Still,* was published by Finishing Line Press and another, *Hieroglyphs of Father-Daughter Time,* was published by Word Temple Press. She co-edited, with Laurence Carr, a collection of works by Hudson Valley women writers entitled *A Slant of*

Light: Contemporary Women Writers of the Hudson Valley which won First Prize in the 2014 USA Book Awards for Anthology and was a Finalist in its Women's Literature/Chick Lit category. Jan's poetry volume, *Foraging For Light* was published by Finishing Line Press in 2019. Her chapbook about Bess Houdini, *Over the Moon Gone: The Vanishing Act of Bess Houdini*, was recently published by Palooka Press.

Kappa Adair Waugh

Born into a family in which everyone – grandparents, parents, siblings – wrote, Kappa grew up assuming that writing was something all people did. She sent off a manuscript to Harcourt Brace when she was 11. Rejected. Kappa's poetry was published in school and college literary journals and, during her twenties, in *BlackRock*. More recently, Kappa's work has appeared in three editions of *Legacies: Fiction, Poetry, Drama Nonfiction (Cengage)* in a poetry anthology, *An Apple In Her Hand (Co-author)*, and in *A Slant of Light: Contemporary Women Writers of the Hudson Valley* (Codhill Press). Her work has also appeared on the poetry blog, *Writing*

in a Woman's Voice, *The Episcopal New Yorker*, *Lakeview Press*, and *Lightwood Press.com*. Kappa recently retired after twenty happy years as Reference Librarian for Vassar College.

Acknowledgements

*Grateful acknowledgement is made to the following publications
in which these works first appeared:*

Colleen Geraghty, "Fisher Queen," *Lightwood Press.com.*

Tana Miller, "A Nobody (Thanks to Emily Dickinson)," *Her Words: For,
About, and By Women.*

Mary K O'Melveny, "Memory Against Forgetting," *Dispatches from the
Memory Care Museum* (Kelsay Books).

Mary K O'Melveny, "Stork Stories," *"Writing in a Woman's Voice."*

Mary K O'Melveny, "Testing the Limits of Art," *GFT Magazine.*

Mary K O'Melveny, "Mourning Dove Portfolios," First published in *Sleet
Magazine*; revised version published in *Albany Poets.*

Jan Zlotnik Schmidt, "We Gather It All In," The Poet's Choice.

Jan Zlotnik Schmidt, "Joseph Cornell and Houdini," *Global Poemic.*

Jan Zlotnik Schmidt, "There is Nothing New about Grief," *Change Seven
Literary Journal.*

Jan Zlotnik Schmidt, "Dream: An Angler at One Hundred,"
Albany Poets.

Jan Zlotnik Schmidt, "Bosom Buddies," *The Broadkill Review.*

Jan Zlotnik Schmidt, "The Glint in Parchment," the *Eastern Iowa Review*;
selected and republished in the Eastern Iowa Review's anthology, *Best
Lyric Prose Plus.*

Kappa Waugh, "God Has a Zillion Refrigerators," first published in *The
Episcopal New Yorker*; republished in *Lightwood Press.com.*

Made in USA - North Chelmsford, MA
1311151_9781735846064
04.12.2022 1621